Anarcho-Punk: Music and Resistance in London 1977-1988

By David Insurrection

Published by Earth Island Books
Pickforde Lodge
Pickforde Lane
Ticehurst
East Sussex
TN5 7BN

www.earthislandbooks.com

Printed and bound by Solopress

Anarcho-Punk:
Music and Resistance in London 1977-1988

David Insurrection

Foreword by Tony Drayton

Contents:

Anarcho-Punk:
Music and Resistance
in London 1977-1988

By David Insurrection

FOREWORD

Punk life

Ripped & Torn was my first fanzine, started in November 1976. I experienced and covered punk bands such as Sex Pistols, Damned, Vibrators, Generation X, and Eater first hand in places like the Roxy, Hope & Anchor and the Nashville. The fanzine really found its voice in covering the next wave of bands, as the music press declared punk was dead and moved onto things less interesting. This left Ripped & Torn as the vanguard of fanzines giving voice in 1977 and 1978 to bands such as The Ants, Raped, Lurkers, Alternative TV, Electric Chairs, Nipple Erectors, Psychedelic Furs and many more.

There was a squatting scene full of punks who had migrated across Britain, Europe and the world to London to experience punk rock, and they adopted The Ants as their figurehead. I was living at the time in a squatted area that declared it's independence as The Free State of Frestonia, so was steeped in the power of squatting as more than just a place to live but a political statement. At the same time I remember walking from an Ants gig at the Roundhouse with a bunch of people and opening squats in a tenement block on Charing Cross Road just to get them somewhere to sleep and live for a while. London was derelict in large parts, and empty/abandoned properties were everywhere.

In December 1978 in Small Wonder Record shop proprietor Pete Stennet gave me a cassette of a group he was planning to release on his record label, also gave me some sheaves of writings done by the group which he said would help explain their stance. This cassette was Feeding Of The Five Thousand and the band was Crass. I was knocked out by the music; it was as powerful as hearing the Sex Pistols for the first time, hearing The Ants for the first time. Then I read their literature and their lyrics which took it to a different level.

Crass also showed what was missing in the squat punk scene, that we were descending and dying in a pit of decadence and missing the point of punk – the anarchist stance, that made it important and vital. I

1

quickly arranged an interview with Crass and published it in the next Ripped & Torn, their first interview. Soon after Crass played at the Music Machine, most of squat punk London was there and from the next day leather jackets started having Crass logos on them next to The Ants. When Adam went on his pop odyssey jacket backs became Crass collages; this was the beginnings of anarcho-punk.

I was there through the developments of Anarcho punk, such as the Wapping Anarchist Centre, Centro Iberico, Black Sheep Housing Co-op, Meanwhile Gardens; squatting warehouse, Fire stations, churches and hospitals as we carried the Anarchist flame, by this time publishing a fanzine called Kill Your Pet Puppy. When David contacted me about his ideas for this book I thought it was an incredible concept but wouldn't be possible; the history too fragmented, places too far away in time and place, anarcho-punk veterans too hard to find.

David invited me to join him as he photographed the houses where Kill Your Pet Puppy was created, Puppy Mansions one and two. As the day progressed I was impressed by his diligence, patience and perseverance. As he spoke of the previous places and people he had covered, and his plans he had for future locations I thought if there is one person who can do this justice it is David.

The book you now hold in your hands is proof that he was the right person to do this, perhaps the only person able to do justice to this subject. It is clear that it is a subject close to his heart. Not only has he dug into his own knowledge, he has helped many people bring out long buried or forgotten memories and incorporated their knowledge and stories into his texts which powerfully give context to the tremendously evocative pictures.

In his introduction David gives his reasons and aims for the book, when he asked me to write this foreward I was worried I would be just be repeating his words so I will just say thanks David again for inviting me to endorse this work, and for creating this work..

It is a very important book to me as Anarcho-punk was always more than just music, though often the music was powerful it was about about people coming together and living as best they could an alternative life outside of society. David has managed to show that here.

Tony Drayton.
Photograph by Zero Baby,
October 3rd 2024.

Tony Drayton/Tony D/Tony Puppy

May 2024

Introduction

In 1977 Crass rolled up to a squatters festival in Huntley Street, London. It would be their first ever public performance. A milestone if you like which would mark the early stirrings of a new scene. However it was the Feeding of the 5000 (released a year later) that would turn heads and inspire hundreds if not thousands across the country to follow their lead. Whilst the old guard had faded - many of punk's first wave becoming absorbed and muted and bought out, this new breed became a harbinger of hope engaging a whole new generation of punks. A call action if you will it became a driver for political change. .

Historically when the possibility of nuclear annihilation seemed all too real, when the State was bent on destroying mining communities and driving up unemployment and flexing its military muscle by sending young men to die in the South Atlantic, anarcho-punk became a vital component in the fight. It fought for life, liberty and freedom for all. It fought for human freedom and animal rights.

Bands, zines, labels and self managed autonomous spaces and houses became the frequency of this new scene. DIRT, Subhumans, Conflict, Flux of Pink Indians, The Apostles, Poison Girls, Toxic Grafity, Guilty of What? Pigs For Slaughter, Kill Your Pet Puppy, All The Madmen and Wapping Autonomy Centre and the Centro Iberico were all major players. New sounds. New ideas. New tribes. A true revolution. Astrid Proll (Baader-Meinhof Gang), Martin Wright and The Monday Group, London Autonomists, Stoke Newington Eight, McLibel co-defendant Dave Morris and the London Workers Group, British Black Panther Movement, the Spanish Resistance, Anarchy magazine and Class War and Stop The City also figure in the story.

With this book my hope is to give people a flavour of the times and the people who lived through those years. I've chosen to tell their story by looking at places, be they music and/or social spaces and squatted houses. It's a fascinating story. I began this journey three years ago spurred on by friends and acquaintances alike. "It would make a great book" Pete Fender (Rubella Ballet and Omega Tribe) told me. Though there were and are regional scenes I decided to focus my research on London. Most people and bands tended to gravitate there after all.

Whilst the book is an historical document of the period 1977-1988 my hope is that it can also have a second life as a guide book. You too can visit these same historical locations should you wish. I've tried to give people a sense of what it was like then today. For example I've shared wherever possible photographs of how these locations look should you visit them today. Sadly some buildings, like for example those that once provided homes and shelter to the Centro Iberico and Campbell Buildings, have since been demolished. As a result I've not covered these in as much detail giving only a hint of their activities. So why not join me as I step back in to the past, once again reliving those tumultuous times.

Some of the quotes I've used have come from pre-existing sources like KYPP. Others from 1 to 1 contacts.

Finally I must give thanks to the following people without whom none of this would have been possible. Steve Corr, Nick Hydra, Penguin, Mark Davess, Dev, Greg Bull, Phil Ritchie, Eliseu Huertas Cos, Nick Evans, Richard Crow, Col Latter, Gerard Evans, Chris Ward, Kevin Thorne, Mick Slaughter, Martin Wright, Boff Whalley, Sean Finnes, Graham Burnett, Deno DIRT, Gail Thibert, Karen Penfold, Ruth Elias, Larry Peterson, Zillah Minx, Nathan Brown, Hugh Vivian, Mick Harrington, John Clifford, Jaz Wiseman, Tony Drayton, Charles Loft, Nick Soulsby, Katrin Parmentier, Joseph Porter, Cristina Mazzoni, Michelle Brigandage, Tom Vague, Kevin A State of Mind, Tim Paine, Bob Short, Sean Forbes, Lizzie Glennie, Louise Challice, Leon Mahon, Nick Antisect and last but not least Chris Low.

Chris Low outside 121 Centre. Photo courtesy of Chris Low.

Wapping Autonomy Centre

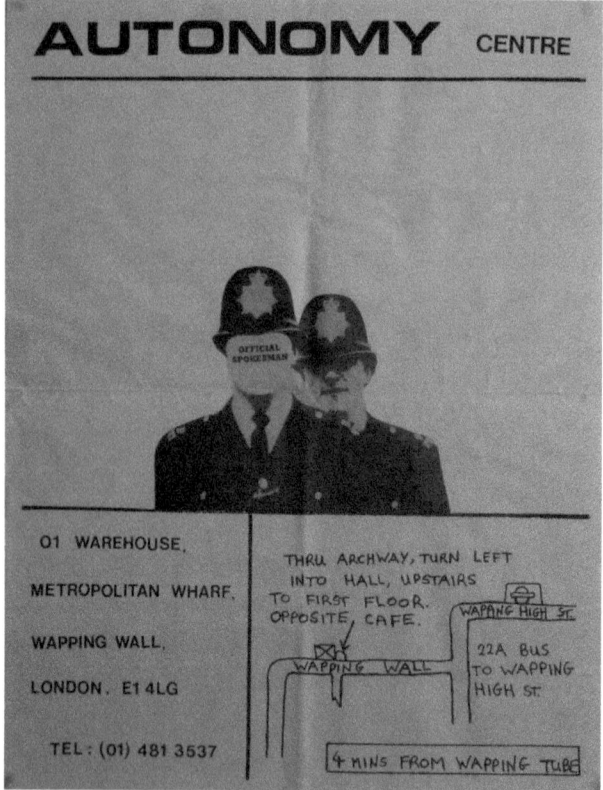

Photo by Michael "Penguin" Baxter

Wapping Autonomy Centre née Anarchy Centre was set up in a 2000 sq ft rented warehouse space in Metropolitan Wharf, Wapping in August 1981 after Andy Martin from local punk combo The Apostles, who as chance should have it worked in the building in question at Little 'A' Litho Printers Ltd, suggested they move in.

Little 'A' was firebombed by fascists in 1985.

Vince Stevenson, Iris Mills and Ronan Bennett (Persons Unknown co-conspirators whose political activities and connections attracted the ire of the British state. In 1978 Stevenson, Mills and Bennett and Dafydd Ladd, Stewart Carr and Trevor Dawton were arrested on charges of "conspiracy to cause explosions". They were later acquitted.), The London Autonomists (Martin Wright, Charlotte Baggins who with Chris Broad was part of the editorial group at Anarchy Magazine, Fabian Thomsett and Ian Rawes aka Ian Slaughter), the Puppy Collective and an assortment of individuals

including Andy Martin (both he and Fabian Thomsett and Apostle Dave Fanning worked at Little 'A'), John Soares (Libertarian Youth), Mark Ripper, Scarecrow and Nick and Grant from Rudimentary Peni banded together to make the Anarchy Centre a reality.

Part funded by the Persons Unknown/Bloody Revolutions split by Crass and Poison Girls (421984/1) which raised £10,000 (UB40 also raised funds by playing a benefit at Woolwich Odeon) it became the focus of the burgeoning anarcho-punk scene.

Over the next five months from October 18th 1981 through until February 7th 1982 a glittering array of bands would perform on its stage. A gig was penciled in for every Sunday. The first gig (October 18th 1981) included sets from The Apostles, Cold War, Twelve Cubic Feet and What Is Oil?. Other gigs would soon follow - Cold War, Anabolic Steroids, Terminal Disaster, Urban Dissidents, Flack and Assassins of Hope (November 22nd 1981), The Mob, Zounds, Luz Y Fuerza (Peat Protest. Ex Primal Chaos and Assassins of Hope. Fod sat behind the kit.) and Hagar The Womb (their very first public performance) December 6th 1981, Crass (who on that occasion went by the name of 'Shaved Women') and DIRT (December 19th 1981), Twelve Cubic Feet, The Apostles, What Is Oil? and The Survivors (20th December 1981), The Sinyx, Assassins of Hope, Flack, Boiled Eggs and Cold War (27th of December 1981), The Turdburglars, The Mob, Apostles, Null and Void, Flack and Blood and Roses (31st December 1981), Part 1, The Witches, The Apostles and Blood and Roses (3rd January 1982), Hagar The Womb, Windy Miller and the Windmills (Tony Drayton), Faction, Flack and Vertical Hold (10th January 1982), Conflict, Rubella Ballet, Seething Wells and Anthrax (17th January 1982), Rudimentary Peni, Part 1, What Is Oil? Slaughtered

Crass at Wapping Autonomy Centre 19/12/81.
Photo by Graham Burnett.

Innocence, Ex-People and The Void (24th January 1982), DIRT, Youth In Asia, Social Diseases, Annie Anxiety and Polemic Attack (31st January 1982), Youth In Asia, The Committed, The S Haters and Flack (February 21st 1982), Part 1, The Witches, Blood and Roses and The Apostles (January 3rd 1982), The Sinyx and Rudimentary Peni (February 27th 1982), The Ex, Flack and Anthrax (February 28th 1982), Naked (February 14th), Youth In Asia, S Haters, Flack, The Committed and Empty Dreams (21st February 1982) and The Snipers, Cold War, Faction and The Assassins Of Hope (February 7th 1982). Alternative comic Tony Allen did a stand up comedy act at the Centre which according to witnesses "went down like a lead balloon."

Leon AOH: "In late 81 and throughout 82 we played a number of times at the Wapping Autonomy Centre and we used to go to there every weekend to watch bands .We became particularly close to Terminal Disaster (who were from the same part of East London as ourselves and like us rehearsed in Alan Gordon's rehearsals in Leyton.) The Apostles ,Hagar The Womb and The Sinyx."

Tony D: "We soon got involved in bringing food and organising a lot of drink to be sold at the events. Brett used to cook vast amounts of veggie curry and we arrived on the tube from Kilburn to Wapping. The drink was driven in by a punk named Gary and his girlfriend, after a couple of weeks of trying to carry it on the tube as well."

The Part 1 performance would appear on a single sided cassette release on Semen Tapes (Semen 001) called In The Shadow Of The Cross in 1982.

The Prospect of Whitby where people would congregate

Cold War "Live At The Autonomy Centre Wapping 18/10/81" was released on cassette by Rasquap Products (RAS 4) in 1981.

Albert Meltzer: "With the punks' money came the punks, and in the first week they had ripped up every single piece of furniture carefully bought, planned and fitted, down to the lavatory fittings that had been installed by Ronan from scratch, and defaced our own and everyone else's wall for blocks around. In the excitement of the first gigs where they could do as they liked, they did as they liked and wrecked the place. Loss of club, loss of money, loss of effort. End of story."

Martin Peacock wanted to move A Distribution from Wapping to Freedom as a matter of urgency due to books getting either damaged or stolen. It was run by Dr Peacock and his wife Carol. A Distribution moved premises to a room on the top floor of 84b Whitechapel High Street, London E1 7QX.

In 1980 Peacock aka "Simon" (posing as a night watchman) successfully

Tonbridge Club

infiltrated NF HQ Excalibur House, 73 Great Eastern Street, Hackney, London EC2. The Front denied the building was their HQ. "Simon" routed this lie. He was later found guilty of conspiracy to cause criminal damage for which he received a six month suspended sentence. The full story was retold in 'Xtra!' January 1980.

Wapping also hosted the first London anarchist "book fair" December 12th 1981.

While Housmans, Freedom and A Distribution had taken part in the annual Socialist Bookfair the general feeling was one of dissatisfaction. So they decided to strike out on their own. Organised by A Distribution on the coldest day of the year half a dozen anarchist publishers (including Freedom Press, Cienfuegos Press, 121 Bookshop, and Pandora Books) set up their tables. The event promised to raise funds for the 'A' Centre. Whilst the 'Big A Sale' was sparsely attended (just 30 people shuffled round the attendant stalls) it was decided to keep the idea going.

On the 26th of November 1983 it moved to a new location - the Prince Albert pub, 37 Wharfdale Road, London N1, one of London Anarchist Federation's regular meeting places with a view to raising funds for the Fed.

In 1984 the Bookfair moved to its new home at Tonbridge Club, 120 Cromer Street, London WC1 hosting two events on November 3rd 1984 and May 4th 1984. Crass did their part by publicising both affairs as well as providing good cooked food. They also managed to raise £150 for the miners.

After this the Bookfair found a familiar home at Conway Hall.

But to return to our story in March 1982 when the centre's occupants could no longer keep up with rental payments it was forced to close.

Both The Wolverine and Class War used postal boxes at C1 Metropolitan Wharf. Box 17 and Box CW. Produced by Steve Sutton, The Wolverine: Gay Voices of Hostility was an insurrectionary anarchist gay newsletter "loosely connected to the London Autonomists/Monday Group - some members of whom were also involved in the early incarnation of Class War. Published in London in the early 1980s." The Wolverine was typeset by Little 'A'.

Interestingly during this same time period the Anarchist Youth Federation (AYF), whose membership included Ian Rawes, Andy Martin, Sean Mason, Assassins of Hope, Peat Protest and Terminal Disaster and The Sinyx, became a hot topic. Leon from Assassins of Hope again: "AOH got on well with Ian Slaughter and we were more influenced by Syndicalism and the Spanish Civil War than many of the other bands in the anarcho scene (at least in part due to the influence of The Apostles)." However it failed to gain traction. Chris Low: "Still, "From small acorns mighty oaks do grow" and Ian and Sean were the only (ex) punks to align themselves with the original London Class War group when that was founded a couple of years later."

Centro Iberico

83a Haverstock Hill

Many of those involved with the Anarchy Centre picked themselves up and moved to new squatted premises - an old abandoned school (North Paddington Lower School which had been squatted by Maida Vale Squatters from November 3rd 1975. The same squatting crew had cracked open 101 Walterton Road, Joe Strummer's famous abode in 1974 which gave its name to The 101'ers) at 421 Harrow Road W9. Known as the Centro Iberico, it had first been established (in its own self managed setting. It had previously met at the Parish Hall of Holy Trinity, Kingsway, London WC2) by Spanish Republican exiles who'd fled Franco's fascist Spain in June 1973 at 83a Haverstock Hill, Camden NW3 before eventually moving to Harrow Road in 1977.

One of its principal movers was Miguel García García. In Spain García had been active in the Spanish Resistance smuggling guns. In 1949 he was captured and sentenced to death. However due to international pressure his sentence was commuted to 20 years in prison which he served at Carabanchel Prison. It was there that he met Scottish anarchist Stuart

Christie. In 1969 he left Spain but continued to spread anti-Francoist dissent wherever he went. He eventually settled in London.

The basement of 83a (beneath a betting shop) became a sanctuary for affinity groups from all over the world including Central and South America and Europe. Whether you needed food and a bed for the night or a place to stay, its door was always open.

The Black Flag editorial collective which at the time included Albert Meltzer, Miguel Garcia, Phil Ruff, John Olday, Ted Kavanagh, Lynn Hudelist, Iris Mills and Graham Rua plus Stuart Christie and his good wife Brenda, met there.

Black Flag was printed in an adjacent room on an offset printing press that belonged to Ted Kavanagh and Anna Blume. Ted had been involved with the Wooden Shoe bookshop, 42 Old Compton Street W1 (1966-1967).

Miguel was always gracious to whoever visited, dispensing drinks.

In September 1976 the Centro was forced to find other premises after the owner of the betting shop upstairs wanted to turn the basement in to a gambling club.

Eliseu Huertas Cos was one of Centro Iberico's oldest and permanent Spanish residents. Chris Low popped him a few questions on my behalf. Eliseu: "As well as being into the scene since the sixties I got fed up with Crowley and psychedelics, all that undercover (Operation) Julie thing going on in the West Country, people going back to the earth and communes. Instead I opted for the traditional political Republican diaspora. I had read a review in Oz about "Franco's Prisoner" so it was inevitable that I would meet Miguel Garcia in London. As soon as I met him I noticed he knew my place of origin in Catalonia, as it had been the scene of the ambush of legendary anti-Franco guerrilla, Francisco Sabate Llopart and his eventual death.

I lived at the Centro from 1974 after it had been taken over by a friend of mine Eduardo Niebla (ex-Gong and Atila) but couldn't live there for long as it had become a dangerous place, having been attacked by the National Front . Also one couldn't sleep there as it was populated by musicians.

Leon AOH remembers: "Once Wapping Autonomy Centre had closed down Assassins of Hope were one of the many people and bands that helped with the running of The Centro Iberico .We used to rehearse in the smaller gig space on the ground floor and organised a couple of small gigs for ourselves and others there in Spring/Summer of 82. We also played the bigger gig space upstairs a few times .The biggest of those gigs was with Amaterdamned ,Zounds, Conflict, Rubella Ballet and ourselves in May 82."

"The Spanish anarchists lived in the classrooms upstairs and allowed us to convert a former assembly room downstairs into a performance space. A stage was built using old cookers from the kitchens covered with carpet retrieved from skips. Although the Centro was evicted at the end of 1982, for a few months during the spring and summer it was used once a week for anarchist punk gigs."

However while the Centro Iberico is perhaps best known for attracting a plethora of anarcho-punk artists to its stage, some of its early musical forays included putting on Rudi, Raped and The A.U.M. band (21/10/78), Rudi, Four Kings and Bitch (05/11/78), Throbbing Gristle (21/01/79), Eduardo Niebla band (30/03/80), Inner City Unit, Androids of Mu and The Door and the Window (10/05/80), Eduardo Niebla and Friends (04/10/80) and Eric Random, Swamp Children and The Wind Up Ensemble (14/07/81).

Some anarcho bands also joined the fray. Poison Girls, Eratics and Disco Students (14/03/80), The Astronauts, Zounds and Drunken Poets (11/05/80) and The Mob, Zounds, The Astronauts and Null and Void (29/08/81).

It also hosted anarchist events - an all-night party to celebrate Joe Hill's 100th birthday anniversary (06/10/79) and an Anarcho-feminist conference (7th until 9th December 1979).

On Sunday the 14th of March Annie Anxiety took along her then romantic partner Wattie Buchan from The Exploited to the Centro Iberico which shook up some of the people there. They cornered him in the toilets and poured the contents of a tin bath containing tea bags and seaweed over his head. Andy Martin: "He was on his own and unarmed. I jumped to his assistance and supported him ... because it seemed absurd to me that he should have to endure a scene from The Sweeney (punk style) followed by an obscure aquatic initiation when all he had done was pay his £1 to see a few punk bands perform.."

Unfortunately the school that once reverberated with the sounds of punk rock dissent was eventually evicted and has since been replaced with a parade of shops.

Al Livingstone: "Punk is/was prophetic - all the words are coming true, we have no future in this wasteland. The Anarchy Centre was just a way of showing that it is possible to create our own lives, to live our own lives.

Listening to a tape of Blood and Roses, a bit of Tony D.'s drunken interview with Bob. "They can exploit me. They can exploit the band. BUT THEY CAN NEVER EXPLOIT THE IDEA."

And that is true."

García passed away in 1981.

Conflict's "Live At Centro Iberico" (XN 2007) was recorded (by Pete Fender and Paul Tandy) on the evening of 13/08/82. It was released on Poison Girls imprint Xntrix Records in 1982. It included six tracks.

· A1 Kings & Punks

· A2 Meat Means Murder

· A3 Exploitation

· B1 Bullshit Broadcast

· B2 Vietnam Serenade

· B3 No Island Of Dreams

Xntrix's point of contact was Rough Trade c/o 137 Blenheim Crescent, London W11. Spiderleg Records could be found at the very same care of address.

The Omega Tribe set 13/08/82 was also recorded and intended for release. However only "Punk Roles" was ever released - on Omega Tribe compilation CD "Make Tea Not War" (SEEP18CD) through Rugger Bugger Discs in 2000.

The Blue House

Sutton House is a Grade ll Tudor manor house on Homerton High Street. It was built in 1535 by Sir Ralph Sadleir, Principal Secretary of State to Henry VIII. It is the oldest residential building in Hackney.

Falling in to disrepair it was rescued by squatters in 1985. One of its original occupants Christine named it The Blue House after her favourite club in Hamburg.

Several bands would play there. Disorder, Slave Dance and Sons of Bad Breath (a benefit for Class War 21/09/85 following the "Bash The Rich" march through the leafy London suburb of Hampstead), Antisect (a benefit for the ALF with The Deaf Tones) and Blyth Power, Eat Shit,

Decadent Few and Flowers in the Dustbin were just some of those who graced the stage there. FITD (on the evening of 05/04/85) were paid in cans of Tennents Super.

Stuart (Belgrano) ran Belgrano's Cafe in the panelled room with the black and white chequered floor.

On the 11th of December 1985 Temple Records and All The Madmen co-hosted a benefit for The Blue House at Stoke Newington Town Hall. Joining The Angels Ov Light (Psychic TV) that night were Blyth Power, The Astronauts and Zos Kia.

The squatters were eventually evicted in 1987. They picked up their things and moved to Laura Place, a Salvation Army property in Clapton.

After a campaign was set up to save it, Sutton House was fully restored and is now in the hands of the National Trust. It was opened to the public in 1994. The exhibition room in the attic was transformed in to a squatter's bedroom to mark the 30th anniversary of when it was squatted. As part of the celebrations on November 14th 2015 Flowers In The Dustbin (the first band to ever play there) plus special guest Pete Fender (Rubella Ballet and Omega Tribe) played at a special squatters reunion party. "If the kids are REunited!"

I spoke to Gerard Evans from Flowers In The Dustbin about the Sutton House 30th anniversary gig. Here's what he said:

"Flowers in the Dustbin had been the first band to play at the Blue House when it was squatted back in the 80s. Returning, courtesy of the National Trust, to play in the mid-2010s, so much had changed.

Not least Hackney. I went off to the offy to buy a couple of cans (that bit had stayed the same!). Taking them to the counter, I could only presume that they'd made a mistake and charged me for a four-pack. On finding out that they were simply taking the piss, I left said cans in the shop & walked bewildered back to the venue.

Luckily, help was at hand in the shape of a temporary bar. They'd made an effort – lots of punky type photocopies stapled to the wall, whilst the women behind the bar had done themselves up for the night to look like Roxy-era punks. They were also selling snakebite and black! Further

Photograph by Michael Baxter

back still, parts of Sutton House felt like a setting for Robin of Sherwood, including the charming courtyard.

Consequently, the whole event felt like some kind of fetishised battle re-enactment. An old friend from my youth tapped me on the shoulder and had turned up, bought an FITD t-shirt, ripped it up and safety-pinned it back together. As had her 3 companions. Embarrassing stuff.

But it was a lovely evening with a genuine sense of reunion for many. Handshakes and hugs reverberated around the ancient building as layers of the past collided and the kids were reunited. We also got paid £500. Cash not lager. The times they had a changed."

The Ambulance Station

Squatted in the winter of 1984, the Ambulance Station became notorious as a venue for live music and a base for anarchist activities. Conflict, Amebix, Antisect (on February 3rd 1984 with Crucifix and No Defences, November 9th 1984 with No Defences, Karma Sutra, Exit-Stance and Sedition and 16th March 1985), DIRT (March 10th with Crucifix and No Defences), Flowers in the Dustbin (March 28th), Chumbawamba (August 18th 1984 and November 17th 1984 with Blyth Power and No Defences), Blood and Roses (April 6th 1985), Conflict, Liberty, Moses Desert Wellies and Public Anxiety (June 17th 1985) and Sacrilege (their set from 1985 features on an LP (UNREST LP068) "Ambulance Station Squat, London, 1985 Plus The First & Second Demos" from 2019) played there as did Nocturnal Emissions (November 24th 1984), The Levellers and Bourbonese Qualk (March 29th 1985).

On the Crucifix/Antisect/DIRT UK tour Tony Lynch shared these reactions in his diaries: "Very nice and rare to see emotions from Punk bands...but after the last date of their U.K. tour (in a squatted Old South London Ambulance station)...some of the Crucifix members were in tears about it all being over and hugged us lot as we'd seen all their gigs etc...Nice, and touching moments...but all too rare indeed in the inhuman punk world."

The Crucifix UK shows were as follows:

Green Man, Stratford, London. Friday 27.01.84
(Crucifix/Antisect/Karma Sutra)

The Richmond Hotel, Brighton. Thursday 02.02.84 (Crucifix/
Antisect/Crux/The Drill)

Ambulance Station, Walworth, London. Friday 03.02.84
(Crucifix/Antisect/No Defences)

Trinity Hall, Bristol. Saturday 04.02.84 (Crucifix/Amebix/Antisect)

St Mathews Hall, Southampton. Saturday 03.03.84
(Crucifix/DIRT/Polemic)

Richmond Hotel, Brighton. Sunday 04.03.84 (Crucifix/DIRT)

Wheatsheaf Hotel, Bolton. Tuesday 06.03.84
(Crucifix/Antisect/DIRT/Mass of Black/Corpse)

Bierkeller, Leeds. Wednesday 07.03.84 (Crucifix/Antisect/DIRT/D&V)

Digbeth Civic Hall, Birmingham. Thursday 08.03.84
(Crucifix/Antisect/DIRT/Polemic)

Vale Social Club, Nottingham. Friday 09.03.84 (Crucifix/Antisect/DIRT)

Ambulance Station, Walworth, London. Saturday 10.03.84
(Crucifix/DIRT/No Defences)

Mark Davess (Sedition from Northampton) joined them on five of
these dates - Bristol, Birmingham and London (Green Man and
Ambulance Station).

I asked Greg Bull (Sedition) if he'd like to share some of his memories of
The Ambulance Station. Greg: "Wednesday 25th January 1984. Antisect,
War Whores, Sedition and Reset to Innocence The Ambulance Station

This was going to be our first gig, after maybe a year of on and off
rehearsing and practicing. None of us were musicians in any way, but

after a year we had picked up some basics and could play simple stuff reasonably well. We kind of thought it was all about the message, but we also appreciated the need to be at least musically competent enough to not drive listeners away.

We travelled down to the Ambulance Station in the afternoon, in a van with Antisect and various friends. I can't remember being nervous, but I probably was, first gig, in London, with a potentially large crowd [I think we were expecting at least a couple of hundred to be there] and I wasn't entirely confident as we had decided to only do three songs. SO this wasn't going to be an epic first show.

When we arrived I was immediately struck by the venue itself, an old converted Ambulance Station [some said it was originally a Fire Station, but to us it was always known as the Ambulance Station.] it was larger than I expected, an imposing Victorian building on the corner of one street on the Old Kent Road. The area in which it was situated seemed pretty run down. But that was always my impression of London in the early 1980s, once you moved away from the centre and the richer areas, generally most places seemed run down. Walking from the tube down the Old Kent Road was certainly quite an experience in those days.

Inside it was clear that it had been deserted for some time, abandoned and left to rot, but the squatters, mostly French or maybe Belgian had made a great effort to make it both habitable and workable as a venue. For example upstairs some of the floors had holes in and you could see through to the downstairs area. I distinctly remember thinking this was fairly dangerous and unsafe.

There were various rooms downstairs that you had to go through to get to the main performance hall, and I was impressed with the organization and dedication that the squatters had put into the building, with presumably very little money. It was all a bit ramshackle but it was what I had expected.

As you walked into the main room, the stage was on the right and probably 50 cm high, maybe and you had to more or less walk past the band on stage to get to the viewing area. When looking at the stage, in the background you could see one [possibly two?] large shutters behind the stage which were where the ambulances [or fire engines] would use to exit. SO this meant the gig area was actually a large garage type space

where the vehicles were stored and looked after when it was a working ambulance station. The ceiling was high to accommodate the vehicles. It was cold, gloomy and dark as befitted a dystopian squat scene and a world threatened by impending nuclear war and the threat of what we considered to be a police state.Thinking about it now the squatters had possibly made the building a less inviting place to be, fearing an overcrowding of punks or other factions who would be able to take over the place. No evidence to suggest this, just thinking back on the place.

My overwhelming memory of that room was how dark it was, I cant remember much natural daylight in there and from memory the overhead lights were on whilst we set up and practiced in the afternoon. Being as this gig was in January it got dark very early and once the main lights were turned off, when the gig started, it was very dark in there. From memory this gave the place quite an atmosphere once the stage lights were on, a very dark audience, silhouetted against the lights on the stage. I remember watching the other bands through a sea of spiky haircuts, dreadlocks and spiderleg crusty hairstyles, they looked like cutout shapes rather than real people.

The crowd was larger than I expected, maybe as many as 300 there, many of whom had started turning up at teatime, kind of 5pmish trying to get in early for free, or simply because they had nowhere else to hang out.

One thing I do really remember was how safe I felt there, able to wander around on my own with absolutely no sense of danger. Everyone seemed happy, positive and friendly, completely different from some punk gigs I had attended in London, where there was at times a brooding sense of impending violence, and in fact cases of fights breaking out. None of that here at the Ambulance Station.

Epilogue.

I revisited the Ambulance Station a few weeks later to witness the mighty Crucifix/Antisect legendary gig there, but the venue hadn't changed much in that short time. However, a few years later I once again ended up at a gig there with my friend Leo Casey and her band. And the place had been completely transformed, the stage was in a different place, the walls had all been painted a bright white/magnolia colour and there were large candles in sconces on the walls, house plants [!] and no punks in sight. The main room had a warm glow about it and it was so much more pleasant than the previous times I had visited. It was a different era I guess."

Bourbonese Qualk were long term occupants. Their tenure there involved putting on gigs and exhibitions. They wrote and recorded two albums at the Ambulance Station - 'Hope' and 'Preparing For Power' in 1984 and 1986. "Our ambition was to create a radical 'cultural–political centre' (though we would never have used that term) and a general base for our activities – performance space, recording studio and office for the Recloose organisation label – in the middle of this piece of un-picturesque South East London. After lengthy renovation (removing 1 meter deep layers of dead pigeons, replacing piping, windows and tiles on the vertiginous roof) The top two stories were converted into artists studios, the middle storey our living quarters. The first floor was taken up as meeting space for anarchist groups, a free cafe and offices for the local squatters organisation, 'S.N.O.W' (who housed more people in 1985 than the local council). The ground floor was changed into a large performance space and bar as well as a recording studio, sculpture studios and print workshops."

On January 14th 1984 Flux of Pink Indians, KUKL and Flowers in the Dustbin raised £300 for the second Stop The City, March 29th. The Ambulance Station acted as a base for operations.

No Defences. Photo by Graham Burnett.

In 1985 The Ambulance Station paid host to a three day festival 30/05/85-01/06/85.

Organised by Bourbonese Qualk "New International Festival" featured the talents of experimental artists Lol Coxhill, Attrition, Current 93, Annie Anxiety and Bourbonese Qualk.

The squat bore the heat of disgruntled locals and nazi skinheads alike as well as attracting the unwanted attention of the police.

The building was abandoned in 1987. It is now an antiques showroom.

The Bingo Hall

The Bingo Hall was set up by those fleeing The Peace Centre aka Rosebery Avenue Anarchy Centre, sick of the infighting crippling the place. Andy Palmer from Crass had a hand in cracking it via a basement tunnel at the back. It was one of a slew of properties in the area earmarked for development.

It functioned mainly as a bar where West Country scrumpy was served in milk bottles.

Blyth Power (and Null & Void) played their very first live gig there on the 16th of February 1984. Joseph Porter: "I seem to recall we had Val and Elaine join us for an epic version of 'The Sound of Silence', and there was no actual door so we all had to climb in through a hole or a window or something to get in."

On the 4th of March 1984 The Bingo Hall paid host to a Crass bill that included Flux of Pink Indians, Annie Anxiety, No Defences and D&V. Flux performed in beachwear and sunglasses. Martin Wilson: "Flux of Pink Indians were performing material from 'Fucking Cunts Treat Us Like Pricks' around the country, around this time and some people had the idea in their heads that we were rock stars. We decided to perform at the Bingo Hall squat in full beach wear, cheekily to add fuel to the Flux 'rock star' vibe that was evident around that time. I do not think the audience that night really got the joke though!"

When an eviction was imminent assorted Burn It Down Ballroom folks retrieved various fittings for use in other squatted properties around the capital.

Today the Bingo Hall is now a major music venue called 'The Garage'.

Molly's Cafe & Blut Blut

Molly's Cafe

Molly's and proximity to Cross Street

Molly's Cafe was a squatted vegetarian cafe at 287 Upper Street. Called Molly Tov's, Molly's and eventually Flob Flobs it was set up by disaffected punk youth following an acrimonious split between two widely divergent factions involved with the 'Peace Centre' in Roseberry Avenue, the anarchist bookshop in Albany Street and 'Stop the City'.

Carl and Tracey Chandler (both of whom resided at 36 Albany Street) were two of the original Molly's squatters. Tracey wrote a book about lesbians and domestic violence called "Lesbians Talk Violent Relationships" with Joelle Taylor and published by Scarlet Press.

They worked in tandem with Islington Action Group of the Unwaged, setting up the Tavistock Square Claimant's Union and Islington Housing Action Group together.

Islington Action Group of the Unwaged (1980-1986) had its own building. The Centre as it became known was at 355 Holloway Road. Not a squat per se. It was leased from the council.

Blut Bluts

Molly Tov comments: "It (Molly's) was previously a kebab shop and many times people came in asking for a kebab!"

The dishes at Molly's were prepared using leftovers from Spitalfields Market.

Tofu Twin Andrew McDonald recalls doing art in the basement, making fish from stuffed newspaper.

Andrew lived with his partner Joshua Korn, Richard Clifford, Roz, Dieter and Tracy Hager at ex-City Lights office building Blut Blut at 313 Upper Street. Blut Blut was named after a ginger tom from a squatted property on Camden Street. His human owner Calvin Sarafyan lived at number 48 along with Jackie Chanzi, Richard Clifford and Tracy Hager and Chantelle from Birmingham. Blut (Dutch) means broke in English.

Blut Blut became North London Squatters Advice's base of operations.

But let's rejoin the story of Molly's. Here's Katrin Parmentier on life at Molly's second time around: "We used to live on the second floor in the summer of 85, kinda after is was deserted by the initial crew and trying to keep it open and running but not being very good at it. I remember me stuffing a marrow with nuts and rice and it being quite the hit on the "menu". I can still picture Alien from Hackney Hell Crew tucking in. but still, the place was a mess. It was much nicer before."

There are reports of Napoleon (Hackney Hell Crew) working there as well.

One interesting point to note: The term "crust" was coined not by Hellbastard but by Ian Rawes née Slaughter following a visit to Molly's in 1984. "I call them 'crusties' coz they look like they're caked in a layer of print on mordial crust."

The establishment of a drinking den in the basement went by the name of the 'Fall Over Club'. Thursday nights were 'Ma Turkey's Jive Dive'.

St James'

St James' or as it became known the 'Grimaldi' church or 'The Parallel Universe' was a squatted church on Pentonville Road. The 'Grimaldi' was where the famous clown and pantomime performer on the London stage Joseph Grimaldi (1778-1837) was laid to rest on his passing.

Al Livingstone : "It was squatted by Islington 'hippies' rather than punks in 1980 (?)."

On the 20th of September 1981 Blue Midnight, Mob, Real Imitations, Dick Healey, Jonathon Brainless (aka J.B.), Staggering Brothers and Murphy Federation played a "Golden Agency Presents" in conjunction with F.O. Records/Street Level gig.

On Saturday the 22nd of August 1981 The Sinyx were joined by Black Flag, Terminal Disaster, Rubella Ballet, and Eratics for a benefit for Parasite zine. That very evening Mike, Leon and Ivan from Assassins of Hope met future Assassins Chantal and Jozi for the very first time. A deal was struck in the pub next door and they joined the band.

On 16/01/82 Rudimentary Peni played. Said performance "The Bile Ball at Kings Cross" was released on cassette.

The Mob played there as did Zounds, Lack of Knowledge, Part 1, Anthrax and The Sinyx (at a 'Fuck the Lyceum' festival 12th September 1982). It was there that Lou aka Louise Harris aka Louise Challice met Mark Mob for the first time. They soon became a couple.

The X-Cretas and DIRT also played there.

It was after one evening on the town at the Hope & Anchor that various Puppies discovered the delights of The Parallel Universe.

Alistair Livingstone writes: "SUDDENLY, SOMEHOW, things changed. Gigs in a church, a squat on the Pentonville Road, No bouncers, no more "them" and "us". 50p to see bands like Rubella Ballet and the Synix and Tinsel jumping up to sing with them. Gigs organised by punks, for punks. Not safe punks in mail order leather jackets. No, this lot were still outrageous, gay punks living in squats, anarchists punks with dazzlingly bright hair and make up. The survivors, the ones who had passed through the abyss. And now they were finding each other again, discovering a network of people and bands and squats and fanzines. A Blood and Roses gig in Stoke Newington. Sitting in a room in an Islington squat, waiting for the dawn and a free gig at Parliament Hill Fields, sunshine, laughter and the Entire Cosmos plus The Mob and King Trigger.

It was all very confusing, so much seemed to be happening, so much was happening. The Wild Youth were on the streets again, a kaleidoscopic frenzy. A celebration. It is true - PUNK LIVES!"

The church caught fire one day and lay derelict for years before getting a new lease of life as a brand new office development.

All The Madmen and 97 Caledonian Road

In 1987 All The Madmen set up home at 97 Caledonian Road on the first floor between Better Badges and Fuck Off Tapes. The building became familiar to people as "Crucial Corner".

Penguin: "All The Madmen went on for about a year and a half until the spring of 1988, releasing the following titles: Blyth Power 'Wicked Keepers' album and 'Ixion' 7" and 12" / We are Going To Eat You 'I Wish I Knew' 12" / The Astronauts 'Seedy Side Of' album / Dan 'An Attitude Hits' album / Thatcher On Acid 'Curdled' album / Hysteria Ward 'From Breakfast To Madness' cassette. Also released were a Mob and a Blyth Power pack with printed record envelopes, which held within; one 12" record and two 7" records for the Mob package. Then one 12" record, one 7" record, a t-shirt and badge in the Blyth Power package. These packages were mainly sold to customers abroad, who did not already have the available Mob and Blyth Power catalogue."

Rosebury Peace Centre

The Peace Centre aka Rosebery Avenue Anarchy Centre, was squatted by punks on September 6th 1983. It was called the 'Peace Centre' after Greater London Council, who owned the property, designated 1983 'Peace Year'.

Amongst those who lived there were Pete Rose (Icons of Filth, In The Shit and Spite), Marina Aniram, Aaron Paul, Katrin Parmentier, Rob, Sarah Lewington (Blyth Power), Spike and Mick Luggy Lugworm. Katrin, Spike, Rob and Sarah lived on the top floor.

Tony Lynch: "The days of the ´Peace Centre´ (in a disused, but now very-used ex-financial building in Londons east-central area called Bloomsbury) were upon us. A lovely three or four story trianglular shaped building that had a great set up with live music in the basement and living places upstairs. We caught many bands play live there..I recall The Mob playing beneath the visible level of the capitals financial arteries streets as a great gig there in the summer of 1983. It was also a very nice place to visit and hang out too.

We labelled them more ´Hippies´ than punks...but now some 30 years on I would say I am more, much more of the latter (if your ´labels´ are

important to you!). It matters not...what mattered was that they were doing something...and doing it very well indeed thank you very little...! I found a camera film there and got it developed and it had numerous faces from its days in '83. Also taking a fair few photos myself too.

The 'faces' in the music world would drift through of course...band members etc. It was a hive of activity....With 'Luggy', Vicky and Mark Mob being faces I saw lots there."

According to newspaper reports there were 20 squatters living on the premises. Buoyed up by their success they were busy hatching plans to start a cafe and a bookshop. The basement was set aside for gigs. It played host to a series of benefit gigs featuring the likes of Chumbawamba, The Passion Killers and Hagar The Womb (11/11/83), Omega Tribe (25/11/83), The Mob and Subhumans and was even raided by the police on the eve of the first Stop The City September 29th 1983. Luggy takes up the story: "I was still awake when they turned up, saw them inching along the front of the building with their shields before kicking in an unlocked front door. There was a strongroom at the back of the basement gig room that we had sealed up to stop punters getting locked in, the dumb fucks thought we were hiding bombs in there!"

Sadly infighting (vegetarians vs vegans) caused many of the original squatters to leave. The centre was closed in 1984 when the vacant office building it occupied was redeveloped. It is now the headquarters of Amnesty International.

The Recession Club

The Recession Club at 22–24 Ponsford Street E9 ran between April 1983 and January 1984. It was run under the watchful eye of Apostles Andy Martin and Dave Fanning and Larry Peterson of cassette label Cause For Concern. The hall, which was hired by The Apostles, was attached to their recording studio next door. Larry oversaw which bands performed there. Those that did tended to be of a more experimental persuasion egged on by Andy who by this time viewed punk somewhat less kindly. Of this he said: "The industrial music scene had taken over and it was here that the original punk spirit had begun to grow and mutate into some huge, many tentacled bat often beautifully subtle intelligence network only occasionally marred by poseurs and butterfly collectors".

Attrition (first London performance) + Coil (first ever performance), Peter North (first ever performance) and The Paramedic Squad (12/10/83 with Assassins of Hope's ex-singer sporting a revolving illuminated bow tie), Paramedic Squad and Lack of Knowledge (16/11/83), The Apostles, Legendary Pink Dots, Nocturnal Emissions, Coil, New 7th Music (this experimental band turned on a transistor radio at 9pm to hear the "pips" at the turn of the hour on Radio 2), Hagar The Womb, Bungle (Assassin of Hope Leon and Larry), In The Nursery (first London performance),

Three Heads Nodding (Thecla & Hippie Kev), The June Brides, Napalm Death, Bet Lynch, Youth In Asia and Condom played as did a variety of poets, performance artists and other industrial/electronic groups.

The Apostles 'Live At The Recession Club' was recorded there 22.9.83.

Unfortunately it's now a vacant lot.

281 Victoria Park Road

281 Victoria Park Road was once home to the infamous hard drinking Hackney Hell Crew from 1984 until 1986.

Andy Martin was a resident 1983-1984. Andy recorded The Apostles 4th EP "The Giving Of Love Costs Nothing" in 1984 after a chance meeting with Simon "Olly" Parish and Martin Barabbas. The release in question is perhaps (according to Andy who had misgivings about it) wrongly credited to The Apostles as neither Dave Fanning or Chris Low were involved. Olly also showed off his fuzz guitar (and bass) playing talents on The Apostles 5th EP "Smash The Spectacle" (MORT 9) on tracks A1 ,A3 and B1. Said record was originally intended to include a copy of Chris Low's anarchist zine "Angry". The Apostles 3rd EP "The Curse of the Creature" at Andy's behest included written testimonies and artwork from everyone living at 281 at the time.

Legend has it that name began as an off the cuff joke one evening in 1983 when Palmer (at '267') requested Mr Tommy Vance play something by Venom on the Friday Rock Show on Radio 1. The truth is perhaps a little less glamorous. Palmer (and Tony Lynch) who thought it would be a hoot to call themselves the Hackney Hell Crew telephoned London's premier rock pirate radio station and record emporium Shades Records with a request that they play something by Venom which they did - "Welcome To Hell". Palmer could be seen bouncing around the attic at 281 hurling fake blood (paint) everywhere. The name Hackney Hell Crew stuck.

'267' was a old four or five storey private house. Its inhabitants included Tony Lynch, Olly, Nick and Palmer and Tarquin and a stripper called Veronique who as chance should have it danced onstage with the UK Subs at The Marquee during a performance of a song called 'Veronique'. Tony was there to witness it. The song in question appears on the Subs fifth studio album Flood Of Lies (FALL LP 018) from 1983.

After 'Venom-Hell-Squat' Olly moved to 281, Palmer moved back to Kent and Nick joined Neil at 'his new squat'.

However in order to discover the origins of the Hackney Hell Crew we need to go much further back.

It's February 1983. Alien, Martin Squarehead, Terry, Aaron Paul and Tony Lynch bond over a love of Discharge and set up home at 75 Offord Road N1. Scrawled across the front of the television set scream the words "....it´s not the work of make-up artists...this TV really does not work"

It's March and Alien, Tony, Martin, Aaron and Terry move to a new abode at 34 Huntingdon Street N1. Living in the basement flat are Stig and gothic barmaid Morticia. Joining them are Dum-Dum, Mark ´Pilmo/Sarge´ Palmer, Cheryl ´Hardcore´ Harding and Karen from Sheffield. Tinsel (Yvonne Linton) from Welwyn Garden City and Jozi (Joanne Forbes) from the Assassins Of Hope were amongst some of number 34's regular visitors.

July and Palmer (from Kent) and Tony have up and moved to 49 Penbury Estate E8 on the fourth floor of a ´U´ shaped council estate block. The Assassins of Hope (Mike Mahon, Chantal Davey and 'Jozi') lived on the floor above at number 12. Mike and Chantal are a couple. Jozi had a white pet rat called Bandit.

281 Victoria Park Road.

Claire Staples (from Peterborough), Tinsel, Cheryl ´Hardcore´ Harding and Karen from Sheffield would often pop round on extended stays.

Nick, 'Kev', Olly (Simon Parrish), 'George' and Al Keating from Woking made a home in a flat upstairs.

October and 36 Balcorne Street E9.

"From the sunny gigs and madness of stumbling upon a new (craze almost!) ´dance´ for punks at gigs...we designed a running up a staircase jauntily in a high-kneed fashion movement...we called this tricky footloose manouevre...´The Disorder dance´...!!!"

Palmer and Tony cracked open this squat. Also staying there were Olly, Nick and Al. The Disorder backdrop hung on the bedroom wall.

Number 10 (on the ground floor) was squatted by Mike and Chantal. Numbers 8 and 12 either side were empty so Tony, Martin, Terry and Palmer and Alien and their respective partners Michelle and Claire moved in to number 8 and Nick, Olly, Al and Sarah from Peterborough moved in to number 12. Metallica, Venom and Slayer were the go-to musical choices of the day.

Skating and BMX-ing was all the rage. Tony and Alien were bitten.

8, 10 and 12 became something of a community if you will. Andy Martin became a frequent visitor after his interest was piqued. However the triad of squats attracted the ire of locals.

Number 8 got a canine pal called Tina. Tina would give birth to a litter of seven puppies at 281.

It's March and our story moves to 5 St Thomas's Place E9. A salubrious setting. Recently renovated. Tony had the upstairs front room, Nick the upstairs back room and Al stayed on the middle floor. They enjoyed visits from Claire Staples, Tinsel, Andy Martin, Alien and Martin Squarehead.

Kenton Road E9. Neil Harding, Tony, Olly, Nick, Al, Alien, Claire and Martin Squarehead slipped in to this property. Ultra-cold. No running water. And an outside toilet. "Alien and Claire 'made-out' to ultra-loud Slayer as the bread bags and bread-tower artwork continued." Al would fashion them in to gloo-bags.

Andy Martin would often pop round as did Deno from DIRT and Drew Bernstein from Crucifix hot on the heels of their U.K. tour with Antisect in February/March of 1984. Drew would go on to become a successful fashion designer. He started his own clothing brand Lip Service in 1985 and passed away August 18 2014.

The 11th of February 1984 and some folks travel to Zwolle in Holland to see Metallica and "Ven-fucken-ommmmmmmmmm".

Mike and Chantal moved to a flat on the fourth floor of a block on the Gascoyne Estate E9. 1 minute away they were soon followed by Tony, Neil, Nick and Al who cracked open a ground floor flat.

Here's Tony with a snapshot of life then: "Tinsel came back into my squat life....kitted out in all black plastic and or leather and long black hair with a lavender streak...the visuals of angel but the characteristic of satan in high-heels....Nick was about to learn this fact! So their 'Dalliance a la 1984' began. We got into ex-Discharge guitarists (Pooch..or Pete

Purtill) new band called ´Helles Belles´ they were pure glam and rock and the singer wielded a long metal sword on stage...not exactly...."Men, Wimmin ennn Chilldrunnnnnnnner" was it matey-mooes..??!!??!"

Tony became a 'dad' to seven puppies.

54 Gascoyne Estate E9. It's late summer. Nick and Tony move to a two bedroom fourth floor flat. High rise living. Lol (Lawrence Maycock) from Margate joined our band as did Melvin from Ashford in Kent. Relations with 281 began to sour. Claire Staples and Tinsel would often pop their heads around the door.

88 Gore Road E9. The next few months were spent in an old Victorian three-storey house overlooking Victoria Park. All the perks including a pay phone. 'Kiwi Kim', Neil Harding, Nick, Tony and Lol enjoyed its palatial surroundings. They struck up a strong friendship with South East London punkers AxYxS. Metallica and Iron Maiden were the order of the day in the house.

73a Lauriston Road E9. Mid-winter. A crumbling four storey edifice. Tony, Nick, Neil, Lol and Al lived in the basement. Kim and her partner Lee moved in upstairs.

And there our story cnds.

The Crew formed an axis of bands that included Sons of Bad Breath (Monti, Martin, Alien and Olly), Eat Shit (Sean, Napoleon, Alien and Olly), God Told Me To Do It (Sean, Bug, Bill and Animal), and the Old Codgers/Blower (Olly, Alien and Martin). Eat Shit and SOBB practiced in the basement of 281.

The Crypt

The Crypt in Deptford beneath St Paul's Church on Mary Ann Gardens, whilst it is perhaps best known for hosting psychedelic nights (every Friday under the auspices of ex-policeman Andy Moore), it also played host to punk gigs from 1984-1986. The master of ceremonies was one Colin Jerwood aka Colin Conflict. Rob Green (Arch Criminals) was the resident DJ. Liberty would do the door and/or the record/merch stall.

Monday nights at 'The Center' at The Crypt featured the likes of Rubella Ballet (November 24 1984), Exit-Stance, Liberty, Stigma, Curfew, Positive Impact, Defyance and Contention (at a punk all-nighter on April 19 1985. Guy Jardine from Stigma set things up. Exit-Stance went on at 3am.), Conflict, Stigma, Exit-Stance, AYS and Liberty (July 30 1985), Conflict (June 30 1985 and Jan 26 1986), Conflict and AYS (January 4 1986), Rubella Ballet and Arch Criminals (January 13 1986), Broken Bones (January 20 1986), Icons of Filth and Anti-System (January 27 1986), Lack of Knowledge and Angels Wear (February 1 1986), Legion of Parasites (February 3 1986), Potential Threat, Unknown Colours and Mentacide (February 24 1986), Disrupters, Revulsion, Free Action and 1waycraze (March 17 1986), Toxic Waste, Exit-Stance and Death Warmed Up (March 24 1986. It was Exit-Stance's last or second from last gig.), Sacrilege, Concrete Sox, The Stupids and AYS (March 31 1986), Liberty, Hex, Virus and The Red Mole (April 7 1986), Fallout, Sons of Bad Breath and Carnage (April 14 1986) and Flowers in the Dustbin.

I spoke to Jaz from Virus who was kind enough to share his recollections of the gig 7 April 1986 with me. Jaz: "From what I can remember, Des Hoskins, the original singer in Virus, secured us the gig at The Crypt in Deptford through his contact with Liberty. We had befriended them November 1985 after both bands had supported Conflict at a riotous gig in Salisbury Arts Centre where the NF/BNP skinheads were beaten and battered out of the venue after starting a mass brawl during our set. The Crypt was run by Colin and the Conflict crew and Monday night was Mortarhate records night. We had appeared on the We Won't Be Your Fucking Poor compilation album but were not very happy with the end results due to not having any of our artwork used and the song we wanted on it replaced with our rather throwaway tune Oven Overture (which Colin retitled The Turkey). It was never really mentioned at the time and when we were offered the gig with Liberty and Hex we were happy to agree to it as we had never played in London before and very naively we thought it might help with getting Mortarhate to do an EP for us.

The gig was three days before my 18th birthday and although Des and Rich Brock (original drummer) could both drive we went up in an old ambulance that was owned by Chris Higgins, guitarist and singer in

Bridport anarcho band Blare. Chris was a real gentle soul, very witty and intelligent and must have offered to drive after I told him about the gig as he was a good friend of mine. Chris came to Gillingham and picked us up at our rehearsal room and I think we didn't take any amps, just guitars and some drum bits and pieces. The old ambulance looked very much like part of the Peace Convoy and we got lots of obnoxious looks in Gillingham as we left for London. I think it had a top speed of about 50mph and the journey took most of the afternoon with lots of stops to stop it overheating. The back of ambulance had been made as comfortable as possible with loads of cushions but we were basically lying on the floor of it, drinking cheap cider and smoking dope. It all seemed to be going so well until we got to London and onto the South Circular – we must have been about 5 or 10 miles from Deptford when the ambulance was pulled over by a riot van full of coppers. Chris was quite panicked by this as they opened the back doors to find us frantically trying to hide the cider and illegal substances. The cops started asking lots of questions, the rest of the band said nothing so as the de facto 'leader' I did my best to try and get us out a very awkward situation. Where are you going? Where have you come from? What are you doing? What type of music do you play? – the usual stuff. I knew The Crypt was home to a psychedelic music night as well as an anarcho punk one so proceeded to spin a yarn about us being a psychedelic band hoping that we might just get off with a caution for being spaced-out hippies as opposed to anarcho punks intent on smashing the state. I should point out that by this time, with the exception of Des, we had all kind of stopped dressing in the uniform, all black anarcho clothes. From the photos that survive, I was wearing a pair of old jeans, Converse baseball boots and a charity shop jumper, Dave a lumberjack shirt and big, black baggy lightweight trousers and espadrilles, Bowz a green t-shirt and a pair of tatty old black, faded army trousers and boots (bloody crusty!), Rich a black shirt and black jeans but looking kind of sensible and Des, the only one with spiky punky hair, all in black looking like what they might have expected. I'm not sure how I managed to get us out it but we escaped scot-free – the band took the piss out of me for weeks afterwards about the psychedelic band thing, especially Rich who said bands like that were notorious for being drug-addled and he thought we'd all get strip-searched when I said that. I have always thought the cops knew exactly what we were and had probably followed us for miles but realised as soon as they saw us that we were a pretty disorganised rabble who couldn't organise a piss-up in a brewery so were not going to pose a threat to anyone or anything.

When we arrived we parked up outside The Crypt and grabbed our guitars and stuff and headed to the entrance. Liberty and Colin were already there so we dumped our stuff but there was a commotion going on in the street – the ambulance had been broken into within a minute or two of us leaving it. Fortunately, there wasn't really anything in there but it did have a window smashed in - pretty eventful and we hadn't even set up stuff!

Colin was chatty and the Liberty lads did the door for a while – I think it wasn't the best turn out crowd wise but there seemed to be people there who wanted to see us. The Crypt was hot, dingy and smelly but that was nothing out of the ordinary. We were at the point where I was beginning to get fed up with the bitchy remarks from the singers in the band and thinking of leaving. I remember the PA playing up but I think that was more for the other bands than us – I don't really have any other memories of Hex or Liberty playing that night. Looking back at my gig diary we got paid £8 for the gig. We imploded a couple of months later when I finally had had enough of constantly being slagged off by Dave and Des - a short time after that Des contacted me saying there was an offer of a Culture Shock, Virus and Hippy Slags gig at The Crypt but I wanted nothing to do with it. The Crypt gig itself is more memorable to me for the fun journey up than the actual gig itself as in what we played. As a venue it was much more akin to the DIY ethic we had in the West Country where we would go to or play gigs in village halls, scout huts, pub back rooms or skittle alleys, squats, fields, garages, etc and that will be something I will always remember about The Crypt."

Action Space Drill Hall and Huntley Street

On the 16th of November 1977 Crass played what would be the first of two gigs at Action Space Drill Hall, 16 Chenies Street, Camden WC1. Built for Bloomsbury Rifles in 1882, The Drill Hall became a popular rehearsal and performance space. Nijinsky and Diaghilev's Ballets Russes rehearsed there in the early 1900s. Action Space arts company took up residence at 16 Chenies Street 1975-1981. It would be only Crass' third public performance and they would be joined on stage by Nipple Erectors and Dead Fingers Talk. Mick Duffield captured this performance on film. .

On May 7th 1978 they would return to play a Rock Against Racism gig, this time with the UK Subs in tow. This would be the first of several gigs with the Subs.

Zounds, Poison Girls and Annie Anxiety also played at Action Space July 18th 1980 and on September 24th 1980 as did Flux of Pink Indians and Poison Girls + Rubella Ballet and The Sinyx on September 19th 1980. On Sunday October 24th, Poison Girls were joined by Rubella Ballet and Joolz. And on April 18th-20th 1984 at an Apples & Snakes Book Launch and Cabaret, Joolz and Benjamin Zephaniah joined a group of poets and musical performers.

16 Chenies Street is now home to RADA Studios.

Adjacent is Huntley Street, where Crass played their very first gig (with Steve Herman on guitar) at a squatted street festival in 1977. 1-9 Huntley Street was then home to the London Squatters Union and 150 squatters and 32 children occupying 52 police flats becoming something of a cause

célèbre. However on the 16th of August 1978 in what has been described as a military-like operation and the biggest of its kind, the Special Patrol Group led by top cop Roy Habershon (Habershon was in charge of the operation to bring members of the Angry Brigade to justice) evicted the squatters despite them putting up a spirited defence.

LMC

LMC or London Musicians Collective at 42 Gloucester Avenue in Camden Town. Andy Martin, in tandem with East London Workers Against Racism, was putting on bi-monthly concerts there September 1982– February 1983. Some of those who graced its stage included The Mob (22/01/83), Kronstadt Uprising, Hagar The Womb and Six Minute War (a benefit for Animal Aid, October 30th 1982), The Replaceable Headz, 4 Minute Warning, Zounds, Rack, Cold War, Twelve Cubic Feet, The Apostles, Flux Of Pink Indians, The Good Missionaries, Youth In Asia, Fallout, New 7th Music, as well as a variety of poets and performance artists. However before that Rudimentary Peni, DIRT, Conflict, The System, Flux of Pink Indians, Living Legends, Subhumans and Annie Anxiety played together at LMC on the 7th of June 1982.

One evening's entertainment was blighted after an incident involving The Apostles and JC. JC (who'd brought along his trusty PA) turned down Andy's vocals during their performance of Pigs For Slaughter. Enraged by what had happened The Apostles cut short their set. In Andy and Dave's minds this was tantamount to censorship. It even demanded a swift retort on "Blow It Up Burn It Down Kick It Till It Breaks" The Apostles first 7" single. That same year Larry Peterson released The Mob/The Apostles 'Live at the LMC" via his Cause For Concern cassette label. CF015/Pacifist PA Promotions!

In 1982 Unite and Reject Tapes released Rudimentary Peni 'Live At The London Musicians Collective 5/20/82'.

Southern Studios

Southern Studios at 10 Myddleton Road, Wood Green began life in 1974 and was the brainchild of John Loder. The recording studio was located in his garage. From the 29th of October 1978 it became Crass' recording studio of choice. Loder and Rimbaud had already crossed paths in EXIT with the two eventually forming a close working relationship. John became the band's financial manager. He's often considered the band's ninth member. He acted as engineer on all of their subsequent releases as well as on those by other bands recording under the Crass Records moniker. He also helped found Corpus Christi Records, releasing records by artists that did not adhere to Crass Records strict ideals and which allowed for a greater, richer variety. The label ran from 1982–1987. John passed away on August 12th 2005. He was just 59.

Nettleton Road

Nettleton Road in the 1980s was where various anarchos would live and play. The first house (number 18) was squatted in the summer of 1981 after moves by the council to rehouse all of the then residents due to the condition of the properties. Following discussions with Lewisham Council an agreement was reached allowing the squatters who by this time had set up Nettleton Road Housing Co-op, to stay there for five years. More people joined. Major renovation work took place on each property, building a viable and thriving community.

Nettleton Road was the birthplace of Colin Jerwood at #8.

Number 5 Nettleton Road was once the humble abode of Si Barry (Flowers In The Dustbin) and one Bob Short (he of Blood and Roses) in the late eighties and Mouse in the mid to late eighties. Mouse aka Sharon Beaumont was a member of the Puppy Collective. She is perhaps most famous for playing bass in Psychic TV as well as in Fire + Ice. Mouse made a recording of The Descent of Inanna with Pinki.

Here Puppy Al Livingstone describes a New Year's Eve party at Nettleton Road: "Year started with a party at Mouse's house (Nettleton Road/ New Cross) where we listened very intensely to first Psychic TV album. Mouse later became a Psychic TV person (played on Godstar single) . Min was also at party, and by September had moved to Beck Road - next door to

5 Nettleton Road

PTV Temple HQ. As per previous blog, Min became Zos Kia singer/ wrote words for song Rape. Zos Kia in turn evolved into Coil".

Mitch Flacko (Hagar The Womb) was once a resident at 11 Nettleton Road, in Ruth Hagar's old bedroom in fact. Karen Hagar and boyfriend Turtle and Veg aka Paul Venables (Hagar The Womb & We Are Going To

11 Nettleton Road *18 Nettleton Road*

Eat You) also stayed at number 11 where there were parties aplenty despite the rather austere living conditions - no heating (which meant hopping around in sleeping bags in the chilly winter months), an outside toilet and rats in the basement. Rent was £6 a week. Roger (the Hags stand-in drummer) lived a few doors away. He helped run the co-op. Karen left after three years after splitting up with Turtle.

There was a food co-op at number 22.

Members of Test Dept stayed at number 8. "The local rag and bone men (look it up), used to come past our squatted house in Nettleton Road (New Cross) and drop off old water tanks, car springs, sheet metal, gas cylinders anything that had a sonic resonance and could be hit with force with metal drumsticks or sledge hammers. This utilitarian approach based on artistic integrity and economic necessity were to form the modus operandi of Test Dept."

Ruth recalls one incident: "We did have a run in with members of Test Dept when we thought they had left their house in the co-op. We shared out what they had left behind including a brilliant record collection and some snakes! It was like Christmas (apart from the snakes). Then they came back and were not too happy - as you can imagine. They nearly bashed the door down and we thought we would be next in line - I'm still convinced we were spared because of the sight of us in the doorway huddled in our sleeping bags!!"

Karen: "I also remember the misunderstanding with Test Department and briefly getting to wear a very cool pair of Seditionaries bondage trousers of theirs until we returned them to their rightful owners."

Conway Hall 08/09/79

Named after anti-slavery campaigner Moncure Daniel Conway (1832 – 1907), this historic building at number 25 Red Lion Square has been a hub of freedom and a place where social causes are discussed and acted upon for 100 years since September 23rd 1929. It is home to the Conway Hall Ethical Society which was founded in 1787 making it the oldest surviving freethought organisation in the world. Controversially (in the 1970s under the Chairmanship of Peter Cadogan) the Society allowed the National Front to meet there. More on that later. It also hosted the

London Anarchist Bookfair from 1985 until 2000 during which time I became one of its regular visitors.

While Crass had played at Conway Hall on three previous occasions without incident - 11/05/79, 26/05/79 (a benefit for Peace News with The Epileptics and Poison Girls) and 24/08/79 (a benefit raising funds for SE London fanzine Toxic Grafity with Rubella Ballet, Epileptics and Poison Girls) as well as after the calamity - 16/11/79 and 02/02/80, it was a gig to raise funds for the 'Persons Unknown' trial on the evening of the 8th of September 1979 that would prove the most controversial.

Toxic Grafity was produced by Mike Diboll. It was because of an unfortunate incident with the police that Crass chose to come to his aid. A Crass flexi including a then unreleased Crass ode "Rival Tribal Revel Rebel" was provided with what is perhaps Mike's most famous issue. It would become the most popular fanzine of the Crass era selling over 10,000 copies.

But to return to our story... Joining Crass on the bill that night were The Rondos from the Netherlands and Poison Girls whose performances went ahead without any visible trouble.

However before Crass could take to the stage, trouble flared. Martin Lux takes up the story: "Around forty plus British Movement skinheads had barged in and were gathered inside the main entrance exuding menace[...] The organisation of the gig had collapsed, Nazis ruled the roost. The only thing holding them back from rampage was that they were waiting for Crass to come on for the finale, then they'd rush and take the stage." From "Anti-Fascist" by Martin Lux Phoenix Press – ISBN 0-948984-35-x The Nazis in question had been drinking in local pubs after an NF meeting at Conway Hall. The Nazis were beaten back by a mixture of Martin's heavy mob aka 'The Monday Group', dissident members of the SWP (Socialist Workers Party) and Anti Nazi League. Eventually the police intervened, clearing the hall of all occupants.

Relations between The Rondos and Crass became strained revolving around disagreements over how violent incidents of this nature should be dealt with as well as who was to blame. Crass stood fast over the use of violence. The Rondos took a different approach: "If there is trouble, we will reciprocate." Crass further stoked the fires believing that the left and not the BM and NF had fuelled the violence.

The events of that night prompted Crass to pen Bloody Revolutions, a pointed attack on the revolutionary left.

Chris Low (Political Asylum, The Apostles and Oi Polloi) kindly interviewed Martin Wright née Lux of the Monday Group on my behalf about the night's proceedings. But first an introduction. Martin: "My name is Martin Wright and I go under the name of Martin Lux. I've been politically involved since 1970 and I started out at the age of 17. Before then I was what you might call an instinctive anarchist. By 1970 I was a conscious anarchist knowing all about what anarchism was, having read about its history, ideology and so forth it being more suited to my frame of mind and temperament. I've been involved in a lot of things but in the nineteen seventies I was particularly involved in grassroots, street action anti-fascism. I was also involved in several publications including Anarchy magazine which I tried to put in a more populist direction which I did succeed in doing to a degree.

In the nineteen eighties I was around when all the great urban disturbances took place. I was also involved in the Class War newspaper from its early inception. I left when it became an organisation. In 1985 we (including most of the London Group) all left as a block because we did not want to be part of a federation. We thought it was better to keep it as a propagandist newspaper. We all got involved again as a group of trouble makers if you like when the poll tax came around throughout many disturbances - in Brixton, Hackney and of course the big one.

The main thing I became involved in was believe it or not Reclaim The Streets which had a very anarchic current to it. It had very interesting groups of people in it. Some were what we might describe as lumpen middle class and lumpen working class. It was a big thing in those days, a very big thing, culminating in the big riot in the City of London in 1999. After that it attempted to keep going and I was still involved in it. We set up the big May Day in the year 2000 for example, but after that it tapered off a bit and went in other directions - in to the Wombles who I associated with and also a more militant form of anti-fascism.

I got involved a long time ago in the London Action Resource Centre and was involved in the Whitechapel Anarchist Group as well which was fairly successful. We had a paper which had a print run of 4-5000. Unfortunately when squatting became illegal it all dissipated quite quickly. Since then I've been involved in a few local things. What I'm involved in now is running the library at the LARC and bringing out a daily videocast (Red and Black TV). And I'm hoping to be involved in stuff in the future once things do actually kick off."

Chris: "What was the state of the far right at this juncture?"

Martin: "It was beyond imagination really but I'll give you a few examples. It was unsafe to be black, Asian or a squatter in any part of London. At any time you could get a brick through your window, or worse you could be attacked on the streets at any time night or day. A lot of it manifested itself in different attacks on people, people posting stuff through letter boxes but also windows being put through. It was really common. It was something that happened all the time. There were attacks on lefty meetings and lefty bookshops but these were uncommon occurrences. They were actually quite rare. There was an atmosphere of fear and intimidation. There was also a reaction to this, an atmosphere of defiance. People wanted to go out and fight them particularly when they tried marching through black areas or Asian areas. People would come out to fight them literally. On some of these occasions serious rioting took place. Lewisham in 1977 is a prime example of this.

Fifty years ago (on June 15th 1974) the first person to be officially killed on a demonstration was killed in Red Lion Square in central London where the National Front marched to have their AGM at Conway Hall and there was a counter demonstration which involved a clash between the police and the counter demonstrators. A young student by the name of Kevin Gately was killed by the police by a blow on the head. No police officer was ever prosecuted for this. That's when the National Front began to get headlines. The amount of intimidation that took place was beyond description."

The conversation then turns to The Monday Group. Martin: "The Monday Group was formed following a quite bizarre set of occurrences. To give you a brief synopsis I met some people who can only be described as nutters at an anarchist conference in Colchester and they belonged to a group called Anarcho Utopian Mystics that was set up by two LSE (London School of Economics) middle class students. They took over the student bar every Monday. I got invited and we got on very well indeed. The mystical component had gone by this point. Disrupting things. Just making a nuisance of ourselves. Showing up the left and the rest of the anarchist movement. A bunch of spineless wallies that they were. What we had were people who were up for making mischief. This we did quite considerably. The only time we did security was on that fateful night but even then it was unofficial. It was swiftly organised.

Crass were doing a benefit gig for Persons Unknown, a group of anarchists who had been, including one person (Vince Stevenson) who had been associated with the Monday Group, accused of preparing for terrorist activities. There was a benefit for them at Conway Hall. Some of the people who had organised it had forgotten to have any kind of security and so on. So I got a ring out of the blue saying this. And I said maybe I can come down and be on the door and take the money. I'll try to take a couple of lads along as well. We turned up. There was no other security at all. Nothing. To cut a long story short about 40 British Movement turned up and just walked in. They didn't pay any money I can tell you. We couldn't stop them. They came in. We thought there was going to be a kick off but it didn't immediately happen because we realised that they were going to get on to the stage when Crass came on. They'd be there hovering around making nuisances of themselves. Some people I know got in contact with some other people - dissidents in the Socialist Workers Party. They were nearby in a pub. They were waiting for this to happen. They were waiting for the BM to turn up. They were contacted about this. They sent someone along to rendezvous and they said that they would be back later and indeed they were just at the right time. With us four people and a couple of other people we recruited and this group, I think there were possibly around a dozen of them, we just went in and did the business. They took the BM completely by surprise. They were tooled up and the results were quite obvious - a massacre. It was the biggest defeat the British Movement had ever experienced."

Chris: "What lessons can be drawn from what happened at Conway Hall that night?"

Martin: "The same lessons that can be drawn from what happened in Lewisham in 1977. There's no other way. They have to be physically defeated. They're not going to be finished any other way."

Finally, what did Martin think of the anarcho-punk scene. "I didn't think much of it but a lot of punks started getting involved in anti-fascism and so on and as a consequence got drawn towards the sort of anarchism as I understand it. The punk scene helped keep the squatting movement going when it was beginning to flag. It was overwhelmingly in my estimation anyway working class which was good. It was the creation of an anarchic subculture which can only be regarded as a good thing."

In 1985 Martin joined his fellow Class War co-conspirator Ian Bone on a brand new musical venture - an irreverent stab at the wedding of Sarah Ferguson and Prince Andrew called "Better Dead Than Wed". "Class War" (A2) was recorded by Caroline K of Nocturnal Emissions one heady evening at 19 Duncan Terrace N1 after watching a Mad Max double bill at The Scala. They'd all eaten hash cookies which only added to the hilarity.

Chris Low who was present wrote the lyric to "Class War" as well as contributing some art to the project. Caroline accompanied Martin (who by this time were a couple) on piano. John Clifford (Conflict) wrote the main riff on "Better Dead Than Wed" (A1) as well as laying down the bass and guitar tracks. It was released by Class War and Mortarhate (MORT 000).

Bruce Kent (1929-2022), who was CND's (Campaign for Nuclear Disarmament) general secretary from 1980 until 1985 and its chair from

1987 until 1990, stayed nearby. Chris fondly recalls Kent, after one uproarious incident at a CND rally in London where assorted London class warriors heckled Kent, offered them a lift home.

19 Duncan Terrace

Conway Hall 19/08/84 and
Paget Rooms Penarth 23/08/84

Nick's garden Penarth 1984

On August 19th 1984, Chumbawamba, Flux of Pink Indians, KUKL and D & V performed at Conway Hall as part of a nationwide Miners' Benefit Tour.

Kev from A State of Mind (Peace Punk band from the Bay Area. They did a split "We Are The World?" with Chumbawamba in 1986 on Agit-Matter Records AGIT 2) kindly shared some of his memories of the evening with me. Kev: "Making my first trip to England in the apocryphal year of 1984 was something I had been looking forward to for months. As a member of the anarcho San Francisco Bay Area band A State of Mind, many of us in the peace punk scene of SF had been greatly inspired musically and politically by the anarchist bands of the UK, especially Crass. I didn't have a set agenda when I landed in London, only to see gigs, and meet the like minded punks who had opened my eyes to the fact that another world was possible, if we were ready to work for it.

Landing in London, things were difficult from the very start. Filling out the immigration card on the flight, there was a question for Occupation....what is your Occupation??

I didn't have one, or even a job. I had been doing anarchist Street theatre for the last few months, so I wrote Actor. Bad decision.

I wound up being interrogated by immigration officials, wondering if I had come seeking work...I assured them I didn't. After an hour or 2, they let me enter, giving me only a 30 day visa, rather than the usual 90. No matter, 30 days was more than enough.

Luckily while I was there, the gig at Conway Hall was happening, a benefit for the Miners Strike. I didn't know anything about the strike, or why it was important, but at some point, someone from either Flux or Chumbawamba explained it to me.

What I did know was that there were 4 bands playing, 3 of them with records out on Crass Records, and in the peace punk community I was part of, anything that came out on the label was a definite record to have.

Flux I was most familiar with, having their album as well as the single, and if I remember correctly, 40 years later now, I had met them through Crass at Dial House, and bonded with them right away.

The gig was a Sunday evening, and I got up close to the stage, checking out the banners that lined the walls of the stage. I forget who played first that day, either Kukl or D+V, and I really didn't know their music that well, but appreciated their presence there. Who knew at that time that Bjork was destined to become a star?

Chumbawamba was fantastic, what an amazing first experience seeing them. A blend of punk and theatre, uncompromising in their beliefs. Each member of the band a show all by themselves. Who knew at that time that they were destined to sort of become famous too?

Flux finished the show, definitely the most driven, most intense band of the gig, and I thoroughly appreciated their intensity, their conviction, and their dedication to not only the Miners Strike, but to the cause of a more sane, compassionate world.

All these years later, I still have no doubt that it was not only one of the best gigs I have ever seen, but also one of the most important. It reaffirmed my belief that the messages of the anarcho punk bands were crucial if the world was going to make it into the next century, and now it looks like that despite our best efforts, the message got lost in all the noise of society.

But for some of us, that message changed our lives forever, and there was no going back ever."

A young Nick Evans arranged the local date in Penarth, Wales on August 23rd 1984. I'll let Nick tell the story. Thank you Nick.

"I was 14 years old. It was 1984 and I was completely immersed in the emerging world of anarcho-punk, mainly the releases on the Crass Records label, which I discovered in a local record shop in my hometown of Penarth, which is about 10 minutes from the capital of Wales, Cardiff.

The shop was called In-Sounds and I bought Feeding of the 5000 and Reality Asylum, a few other Crass Records releases, one of which was Neu Smell by Flux of Pink Indians.

Flux of Pink Indians introduced me to the idea of vegetarianism and not abusing animals and I was very affected by the songs and the words contained on this Crass Records release. As a result of this I contacted Colin Latter, Cölsk, the singer from Flux of Pink Indians and we developed a friendship over the telephone. I would ring him up and ask him questions and he would be very accommodating and very interested in discussing vegetarianism, pacifism, anarchism, animal rights in general and when we spoke several months prior to 23rd August 1984, he informed me that Flux of Pink Indians, Chumbawamba, D and V and an Icelandic band called Kukl would be touring the UK and playing in various village halls and social clubs on a benefit tour for the striking miners who had really been subjected to the wrath of the Thatcher government whose central tenet seemed to be a hatred of working class solidarity.

My parents were committed Labour voters, both of whom came from working class parts of Wales. My father from Synghenydd, which was a town close to Caerphilly, my mother from Town Hill in Swansea.

When I suggested to them that despite my being only 14 years of age we should promote a concert in Penarth and host these bands in our semi-detached suburban house they were not completely opposed to the idea, largely as a result of their being in support of the Striking Miners.

My father lent me £80 I remember, so that I could book the Paget Rooms in Penarth for the 23rd August 1984 and Cölsk told me that the band would be traveling all together on a converted bus, and bringing their own PA system.

So the only outlay that I had to find funds for was the renting of the hall and printing up some posters.

So I went ahead.

I seem to remember booking the Paget rooms in Penarth was a very easy

thing to accomplish. I then waited for the day to arrive and finally they all showed up as promised on a single-decker converted bus.

There were probably about nine members of Chumbawamba, between eight and ten people involved in the Kukl group, one of whom was a very young Björk, (who as you know went on to be a very celebrated and unique globally loved singer) and Flux of Pink Indians who were round about another seven or eight people, D and V who were comprised of drums and vocals, there was a fanzine writer called Phil Hedgehog, the bus driver and PA guy, and last but not least myself, Matthew, Dean and Tom, we were Slaughter Tradition. Slaughter Tradition being our high school anarcho-punk band who sang largely about animal abuse, the end of war and the quest for freedom.

I had printed up maybe 50 posters and put them all over Cardiff, Penarth, Dinas Powys, Barry, Sully and in the window of Spillers Records and maybe a few other shops.

The hall was quite big, I think it contained enough space for maybe 200 people. The Paget Rooms is an old age people's function hall generally, it had brocade and velour fittings, deep red curtains and a wooden dance floor. We'd seen local punk bands there, the likes of the Torture Reptiles and the Innocence and various rockabilly bands like Nervous Breakdown, I believe Shaking Stevens had played there a few times and Welsh hippy rockers, Man, but normally it was used for jumble sales and these kind of events as Penarth was largely known as a retirement destination for older people because it had a very pretty seafront and lots of gardens and quite a nice little town centre.

The evening of the concert the town filled up with spikey haired, black clad punks from all over Wales as well as people traveling from gig to gig all over the country. Local residents seemed surprisingly happy about the whole thing.

Our band Slaughter Tradition played first and we must have played around ten songs. I played a little bit of acoustic guitar and also banged a wooden stick with hundreds of bottle tops nailed into its length which made everyone laugh a lot. I have memories of Einar from Kukl who went on to be in the Sugarcubes with Björk saying to me "well that was pretty good but let me show you now how it should be done" Kukl went on and of course Björk's voice stole the show, this incredibly beautiful, soaring, bewitching, Icelandic, sound coming out of this tiny little human was really extraordinary. It was accompanied by this very avant-garde, soundscape-y gothic music made by the band all of which was punctuated by Einar's strange yelping yowls. It was like an ancient, primeval incantation. Unforgettable.

Then I believe D&V played their innovative proto-rap - anarcho-punk freed from the rock n roll shackles of guitars and bass, just the sound of Jeff's voice on top of I believe it was Andy's quite imaginative drumming.

They were followed by Chumbawamba who were innovative and intelligent largely because they incorporated a theatrical element including wearing televisions on their heads and various slogans and teachings written on their t-shirts and on their bodies in red paint one of which I remember being 'the music's not a threat but action that music inspires can be a threat.'

I found that very powerful as well as their music which was influenced by the Crass Records sound but had another dimension in that they used vocal harmonies and switched instruments having more in common musically with the Fall or the Au Pairs than Discharge or Crucifix, or any of the more straight-ahead one-two-three-four punk bands of the time.

And then on came Flux of Pink Indians, who were playing material from the Fucking Cunts Treat Us Like Pricks record, which was a much more avant-garde, demanding, cut-up style, industrial noise/ jazz sound than their previous record, which we'd all loved so much, 'Strive to Survive, causing least suffering possible' and this was a bit of a visceral shock. They were testing their audience's ability to break free from the rock n roll format and push the boundaries of acceptable music to the limits.

The bands were playing in front of all of these really incredible backdrops of which Slaughter Tradition also had a couple included in this massive display of pieces of provocative artwork which went all around the walls of the hall transforming the place into something akin to a political rally than a concert.

I think maybe 200 people came and I seem to remember donating a couple of hundred pounds to the striking miners.

That night Kukl all camped in a big tent in our garden and the rest of the groups found places around the house on the floor to put their sleeping bags. I have a vivid memory of Bjork sitting in my parents' living room crocheting with one needle, making all sorts of knitted garments and being very quiet and self contained.

Chumbawamba all being northerners, were chatty and very outgoing. I went on to spend a lot of time with them when I moved to Leeds some years later. I even sang a bunch of songs on a double album that they made under the name of Sportchestra.

I remember the beginnings of a friendship with some of the people in Flux of Pink Indians, which continues to this day. I would visit them at their house in Forest Hill and go on motor bike trips with Cölsk and hang out in the TeePee in their garden. I went on to work with Derek Birkett, the bass player, who had a record company called One Little Indian, which is now One Little Independent.

Derek invested in my record label Elemental Records and we had some success with Rocket from the Crypt, Drive Like Jehu and Alabama 3 much later on in the late 90s, early 2000s.

So my friendships with some of these people has endured. I'm still in contact with some of the Chumbawamba people and Colin from Flux of Pink Indians has remained a good friend. Also Einar from Kukl is still friendly to this day in 2024.

I think it was a particularly interesting time because it marked the moment where anarcho-punk shifted from being solely concerned with a certain selection of issues, like anti-war and pacifism, animal rights, and a notion of anarchism or freedom that was a little reminiscent of the hippies' idea of dropping out.

I think that Chumbawamba, Flux and Kukl and D and V doing this tour for the Striking Miners gave all of us a sense that this was a bigger problem really than just anarcho-punk against the world and that it really was the elite or the rich people of the world who were declaring war on the poor people and that if we didn't defend and stand up and make our voices heard for the striking miners then it would be us next. As Flux declared from their record sleeves 'there is enough for all of our need but not for all of our greed'.

Indeed in many respects that prophecy is coming true as the ongoing march of what can only be described as a global theft by the ruling classes and oligarchs to make the rest of the population of the world powerless, poor and subservient.

I remember being very moved by the whole experience which in many respects shaped a large part of my life. The political perspectives changed me and I've been basically a proponent of working-class solidarity ever since."

Nick Evans- Eindhoven 9/6/24

I approached Boff, then a member of Chumbawamba, to add his observations. Thank you Boff.

Boff: "By mid-1984, from the vantage point of our shared house up in Yorkshire (and far from the hubbub of the London squats, zines and scenes), we were beginning to see the anarcho-punk scene fracturing along stylistic lines, with out-and-out hardcore punk heading one way and post-punk experimenting veering another. Of the latter, some of those experiments showed up in this motley assortment of bands touring in support of the striking miners.

Bjork. Photograph courtesy of Kevin A State of Mind

There's so much context to this tour, and to those times, that it's hard to know where to begin. I wonder if all the bands on the tour were asking themselves the same "what do we do next?" question that we were asking ourselves, having seen Crass disband and a lot of bands getting heavier, faster, drunker and dirtier. Penny Rimbaud and Eve Libertine were busy making an album ('Acts of Love') of orchestral synth and poetry, The Mob were getting melodic and dancey, Blyth Power were getting stuck into punk-folk, and my favourite bands at the time – No Defences, Karma Sutra, Poison Girls, Moet the Poet – just didn't seem to fit the anarcho-punk straitjacket.

Of the bands on this 1984 tour, Flux were asking questions, for sure – they had just made their 'Fucking Cunts' album which they knew was partly daring and confrontational and partly unlistenable. KUKL were dabbling in Icelandic sorcery and challenging any punk orthodoxy with whoops and yells and tribal beats. D&V were flirting with a sort of Sheffield council estate rap which was bloody marvellous live but somehow lost its energy on record. The whole time seemed to be a sort of unresolved tail-end of an incredibly energetic movement.

When the miners went on strike in 1984, us lot in Chumbawamba took a long hard look at it before realising that these people on strike were the same people we'd grown up with in our home towns (Barnsley, Burnley, Billingham) – working class families being picked on and victimised by the political elite (not just Thatcher, but Labour's front bench too). We did what a year earlier would have been unthinkable and joined forces with our local Leeds West SWP group to set up a miners' support group, rattling buckets every other day on the shopping streets to raise money for the food kitchens in the pit villages.

We twinned with Frickley and Hemsworth in South Yorkshire and used our band van to ferry food and people down to the miners' welfare hall and to join the early-morning picket lines.

This wasn't seen at the time as part of the anarcho-punk scene – we were having arguments with punks about whether we should be supporting the strike at all. When the idea for the tour came up, we knew there would be people who didn't go along with what we were trying to do. Fair play to Flux for sticking their neck out as the 'name' band on the tour, for gathering the PA and stage crew who would set up each gig on the tour. I can't remember where the bus came from, but it was a bit of an old heap and seemed to break down every other day. Still, the camaraderie between the bands was brilliant, inspiring, and fun. KUKL were a little stand-offish for a while, having just arrived from Iceland into this messy heap of black-clad anarchos, but they soon settled in and we really did, for those brief couple of weeks, become a happy family.

The Conway Hall in London – the venue for the first gig – was always a strange place to play, with its history of political rallies and lefty gatherings, which sadly had been superceded by a more recent history of fascist dickheads turning up for a fight. This gig had its share of skirmishes but nothing too ridiculous. My main memory of the first night is unsuccessfully trying to have a friendly conversation with KUKL's guitarist, who called himself God Christ and refused to engage in small talk. The rest of the band were mercifully more welcoming.

We staggered around the country on our rubbish bus, half-imagining we were a sort of anarcho-punk version of the Pistols/Clash Anarchy Tour, but that image didn't survive the half a mile we all pushed the inert bus along the hard shoulder of the M1 to get it to a garage at a service station. Rock 'n' roll!

The Penarth gig in Wales I remember better because it was organised by Nick, then a young teenager who sang with Slaughter Tradition (who also played the concert), armed not with a guitar but with a rhythm stick made of a broom handle and some bottle tops. We slept on the floor at his parents' house – they were lovely, lovely people – and celebrated what seemed to be an increasingly successful tour. We later became good friends with Nick, and there are photos of the mob of bands on the tour laughingly gathering for an informal photograph in Nick's back garden: they look like nothing less than a gathering of the Bash Street Kids.

The success of the tour, for me, rested on the idea that every gig had its arguments and debates with the audience, with punks who just wanted Flux to play 'Tube Disasters', who couldn't understand Bjork's staggeringly beautiful whoops and Einar's dissonant screams, who wondered why D&V didn't have guitar and bass like a real band, who thought Chumbawamba were just painfully awkward musically – and what was all that dressing up on stage? Added to this were the handful of audience members who would question our support of the strike. This wasn't in the rule book, anarcho-punk was meant to be pacifism, animal rights, anti-war. And it was meant to be loud and angry...

Thing is, we were angry. All of the bands on the tour were angry and motivated and passionate about what we were trying to do. And frankly, by the rear end of 1984 we were questioning the anarcho-punk stylings precisely because we all believed in it so much, we wanted it to change and grow and diversify, not stagnate.

Back in Leeds, we were striking up uneasy friendships with bands like Mekons and Three Johns, with fanzine / NME writers Seething Wells and James Brown, trying to expand our music outwards from a sort of melodic version of Crass and into a hotch-potch of folk, punk, pop and acapella harmonies. When the bus dropped us all off at the end of the short tour and we returned home to our big old Victorian squat in Leeds, we discovered that the entire tour – mainly because of petrol and bus repair costs, as well as trying to feed that many people for a fortnight – had made less profit for the striking miners than we were making in a weekend shaking our buckets outside supermarkets. It didn't matter. What was important was the experience of trying to stick up for people and to take that message of solidarity into places where it was unfashionable. I'll be forever grateful to the members of Flux for having the idea in the first place.

Within a year we'd given up hope of releasing a Chumbawamba record on Flux's Spiderleg label (as we'd been kind of, sort of, vaguely promised) and instead self-financed our own Agit-Prop label to put out our first single, 'Revolution'. The theme of the EP was to step outside the boundaries we create for ourselves and to collaborate, reach out, widen our political and cultural worldview.

Recently I went back to South Yorkshire to see a musical about the miners strike being performed, a musical I'd written over ten years ago and performed by Red Ladder Theatre Company. In the audience were former miners and their families, people who'd seen their communities decimated by their defeat in that strike. The couple sitting next to me had this to say – "This used to be a proper little town. Now there's nothing – after the pit closed, everything just went. And the drugs came in." It reminded me how important those times were to all of us, how much we learned from being involved; and it reminded me of those couple of weeks of travelling around Britain making the case for these people and letting them know we supported them."

Boff Whalley, July 2024

The Chumbawamba and Flux of Pink Indians sets at The Conway Hall were recorded and released on cassette by Acid Rain Products (AR9) in September 1985 though the date (20/08/84) is listed incorrectly.

Thames Poly

Thames Poly (Woolwich SE 18) played host to regular anarcho-punk gigs courtesy of Colin Jerwood between the years 1984 and 1988. These took place every Tuesday night between 8pm and 11pm. Most gigs were in the downstairs cellar bar with the occasional larger affair upstairs in the main hall. Liberty would muck in and do the door.

Those bands that did play included The Partisans (December 17th 1983), Omega Tribe (18/01/85), Conflict + Rubella Ballet and Reality (Sept 5th 1984), Poison Girls (Sept 29 1984), Hagar The Womb (Sept 28 1984), Liberty, Union of Fear and Fata Morgana (January 12 1985), Liberty, State Hate, Stigma, A.T.N. and Pete Dog (February 16 1985), Liberty, Karma Sutra and Stigma (April 12 1985), Conflict, Icons of Filth, Lost Cherrees and Liberty (a benefit for the ALF 24/05/85), Brigandage (June 1st 1985), Conflict, AYS, Exit-Stance, and Liberty (30/07/85), The Three Johns and Hagar The Womb (a miners benefit 28th September 1985), Blyth Power (April 4th 1986), Conflict, Exit-Stance, Potential Threat, Liberty and Admit You're Shit (April 26h 1986. Benefit: Anti-Apartheid), Conflict, Oi Polloi and Shrapnel (Oct 17 1986), Potential Threat, Oi Polloi, AYS, Exit-Stance, AOA, Shrapnel and Chumbawamba (December 20 1986 + October 30 1987, December 10 1987 and December 14 1987), Snuff, Oi Polloi,

Axegrinder, Wat Tyler and Epidemic (a benefit for South London Hunt Sabs put on by Daryl Dixon on October 14th 1987), Culture Shock and Hagar The Womb (July 24th 1988) and finally Steve Ignorant Banned + Reputations In Jeopardy and City Indians (July 25 1988).

Communicate!!!! (Live at Thames Poly), a double LP was released in 1985 and on CD by Overground Records in 1992 and included live performances from the likes of Conflict (The Guilt and the Glory), Liberty (As Fools Rush In), Toxic Shock (Dancing in the Park), Poison Girls (Rockface) and The Ex (M.M.M. Crisis) recorded between September 1984 and July 1985. The whole affair was put together by Leigh Goorney who was the Social Secretary at Thames Poly throughout said period.

Conflict's live set October 17th 1986 was recorded for posterity on cassette and released by Homebrew Music in 1986.

Thames Poly moved premises in 1992

Acklam Hall

Acklam Hall, 12 Acklam Road, London W10 5QZ. Under the Westway flyover. The Acklam community hall opened its doors on the 12th of July 1975. Those who were there were greeted to a set by The 101ers. The following year (on October 15th) Joe Strummer returned to Acklam Hall this time with The Clash, who though they were billed to play alongside Spartacus R and Sukuya at a high profile benefit for Notting Hill Carnival defendants, didn't. Joe is quoted as saying "It wasn't our riot, though we felt like one." They did eventually play a sparsely attended secret gig on Christmas Day in 1979. "Anyone wanna see The Clash? 50 pence" came the cry. UK Decay were the support.

They would be joined by Crass on the 29th of September 1978 supporting Teresa D'Abreu and Pearly Spencer. Crass would play there three times altogether returning on the 26th of March 1979 with The Wall and Poison Girls (a benefit for Anarchist Black Cross and Cienfuegos Press) and on the 29th of September 1979. Cienfuegos Press was an anarchist publishing house set up by Stuart Christie aided and abetted by his wife Brenda.

Two weeks later on October 15th the Weird Tales tour rolled in to town with The Mob, Zounds, Androids of Mu and The Astronauts.

On February 3rd and February 21st 1980 Zounds, The Mob and Androids of Mu played two shows at Acklam Hall.

On the 18th of October 1980 The Entire Cosmos, Blue Midnight, 012, Danny and the Dressmakers, Androids of Mu, The Astronauts and The Mob played at an all-day concert followed by (on the 20th of December and proudly presented by Street Level and Fuck Off Records) a free Christmas gig and pantomime featuring music by Blue Midnight, The 012, The Hamsters, Murphy Federation, Brian Brain, Androids of Mu, Entire Cosmos, Vince Pie and the Crumbs, The Voletones, Graham Drongo and Alan Dogend with the Acklam Halamanic Orkestra.

Acklam Hall became a popular music venue hosting gigs by the likes of The Raincoats, Joy Division. Rema Rema, Crisis (who on the 29th of June 1979 played at an RAR gig at the North Kensington Rock Against Racism Club. BM skinheads attacked the gig en masse. Crisis and their fans beat them back) and Here & Now.

In 1989 Acklam Hall changed hands and was renamed Subterania by Vince Power from the Mean Fiddler. It's gone by different names and guises since then and is currently closed.

Meanwhile Gardens

Stage and crowd area

In 1976 Meanwhile Gardens was rescued from the rubble by sculptor Jamie McCullough who decided to turn these four acres of what amounted to a derelict wasteland in to a community garden. The permission (by Westminster Council) to do so was given a temporary go ahead hence the gardens name.

The gardens (between 1977 and 1988) hosted 'idiots picnics'. These were organised by Lancaster Music Co-op.

On March 10th 1979 the 'If It Ain't Worth a Fuck - Fuck Off' Free Tour splashed down with Zounds, The Astronauts, Psycho Hamsters and Danny & the Dressmakers and on March 24th with Psycho Hamsters, Danny & the Dressmakers, Aqua, The Dogends, The 021, Zounds and The Sell-Outs.

On the 6th of July 1980, The Astronauts, Androids of Mu and Nik Turner's Inner City Unit played there to an adoring crowd.

And on the 19th of September 1981 Blue Midnight, Mob, Real Imitations,

Dick Healey, Jonathon Brainless (aka J.B.), Staggering Brothers and Murphy Federation played a "Golden Agency Presents" in conjunction with F.O. Records/Street Level gig.

Three years later on the 25th of June The Mob joined the merriment as they did on August 6th 1983. Then on the 16th of June 1984 Blyth Power paid what would be the first of five visits to the gardens. On the 23rd of June they were joined by Omega Tribe. They returned the following year 10/08/85 and again on 29/06/86. And on the 25th of July 1987 they played once again, this time with Blue Midnight and Idiot Strength.

I asked Steve Corr (Idiot Strength and Blyth Power), Joseph Porter (The Mob, Zounds and Blyth Power) and Hugh Vivian (Omega Tribe) about their memories of Meanwhile Gardens.

First here's Steve: "My first trip to Meanwhile gardens saw me hitching with my then girlfriend up from Bristol in 1986 to see Blyth Power.

Hitchhiking, being the precarious thing it was, was no guarantee of a timely arrival and consequently we arrived just as the whole thing was closing down, having missed all the bands. I don't think I'd ever heard of Meanwhile Gardens prior to that, but I liked its name, which sounded almost Pythonesque. I thought it must have been made up for the festival.

Little did I know I'd be playing there the next year in the band I'd travelled to see, along with my own band Idiot Strength, appropriately playing one of The Idiots Picnics.

I remember being surprised and disappointed at the low attendance, especially as it was free. It felt like quite a few of the people there had just drifted in to see what the fuss was about.

I was a great setting, nestling under the bridge of Great Western Road, I could see people on buses and on foot gawping at the drugged-up weirdos down below.

The Idiot Strength performance was pretty bad as I recall. It took us ages to get started due to having to eject some really annoying old guy who seemed under the impression that we needed a backing vocalist, or lead singer even. The cheek of the man.

I think this was either my second or third gig with Blyth Power and watching the Blyth Power footage we seem pretty well rehearsed."

Joseph: I have a few vague memories of Meanwhile Gardens – some amazing afternoons watching some great bands and acts. As Protag – then our bass player – was often doing the PA I occasionally found myself lending a hand at set up, during the course of one I remember we fell foul of the garden's designer. The landscaped part we would play in was effectively a circular bank around a sandpit, with a gap allowing a path through to the rest of the park. We habitually erected the stage in this gap as it was both the logical and perfect place to locate it, so everyone could sit on the banks and enjoy the music. It seems the designer had not been consulted as he had designed it as a uterus, and we were blocking the vulva with our stage. I'm not sure how he was eventually placated but I don't remember moving the stage.

One time the police turned up. Two coppers came onto the site to arrest someone for possession, which of course elicited an animated response from a number of the crowd. Within seconds more police than had any right to be loitering in adjacent side streets at taxpayers' expense arrived and finished their business. There was a short melee, but inevitably they won. I do recall one left his helmet behind and had to return and collect it from the front of the stage while the Androids of Mu smiled beatifically at him. He got a round of applause. All fine and funny – but it was surprising how quickly they arrived …"

Hugh: "I went to Meanwhile Gardens a fair few times, I couldn't tell you how many. This would have been 1980/1/2/3/4. I remember that the events were free and held during the afternoon. I'm afraid I'm a bit vague on much of the detail, but here are some things I remember well.

Ted Chippington, who went on to bigger venues, a solo act amongst the bands. 'I like to rock for three days, because it's exciting, don't like to rock for two days, cos it's not exciting enough', impro comic stuff, was very funny! A couple of terrible gags; 'was walking down the road the other day when this hippie came up to me, hey man, want to buy some grass? No thanks I've got crazy paving'

I remember people out of Here and Now, actually it was the drummer, singing about addiction 'and the biggest addiction of all is death!' Which the other watching members of Here and Now laughed at.

There was a great little band that Andy was in, were they called Blue Midnight? Brass section, very cool 'I've got a ticket to heaven, it's burning a hole in my hand'

Androids of Mu, Astronauts, I don't remember any full on punk bands there, although maybe I didn't go to those! Mob and Zounds but they aren't punk bands in the modern, conservative sense.

I remember a group of bikers getting smashed and clashing with a group of West London hippy punks, the crazy colour people were play fighting and this greaser decided to put one in a wrestling hold, completely horrible unnecessary violence so beloved of greasers. I think the victim was a slim Scottish guy.

Grant Showbiz, Null and Void also featured.

Lastly I remember the Nottingham Hill carnival in 1984 (probably) put a big stage in the gardens and Poison Girls were due to play but we had to wait for what seemed like hours for an interminable Aswad sound check, sucked a bit of the energy.

Overall a great place, scene of (mostly) very happy times."

Hope & Anchor

The Hope & Anchor on Upper Street N1 became a focus of dissent and punk rock for three months in 1985.

While the 1970s proved a fortuitous time for The Hope & Anchor, hosting many of the pub rock and punk rock glitterati of the day including Crass and Poison Girls 14/07/79 not to mention Johnny Ramone finding Sid Vicious in the bathroom with a syringe in his arm, the 1980s were less kind. It fell on hard times and was forced to close.

However in September 1985 squatters moved in and set about shaping it to their means. They installed a theatre and a cafe. Conflict's Big John Clifford reconnected the electricity supply.

During that time (between September and November) various bands including Conflict (03/10/85 and 03/11/85), Soldiers of Destruction and Shrapnel (31/10/85), Antisect and Disorder played in the hastily prepared basement area and on 15/11/85 and 16/11/85 on what promised to be a two day event at the Hope & Anchor turned out to be just one after a stabbing incident outside on the Friday evening. On the bill were Conflict, Liberty, Exit-Stance and AYS with all monies going to Stonehenge (15/11/85) and the Bust Fund and Greenpeace (16/11/85). The Old Bill kept a close eye on proceedings. The atmosphere was tense after the Broadwater Farm riot only weeks before. Dabble takes up the story: "I have vague memories of a gig when it was squatted. I think it was around 1985. The gig I went to was Conflict. The pub was absolutely rammed, you couldn't fit another person in the place if you tried. must've been about 400 squeezed into such a small venue. Colin Jerwood (Conflict vocalist) was standing on a table in the bar area, with baseball bat in hand, trying to calm the fighting punks down, as he did not want the cops entering the building - he got his wish. The gig was around the time of the Broadwater Farm riots in Tottenham, as Colin Jerwood, all through the Conflict set, kept making comments about the death PC Blakelock."

Gail Thibert from Lost Cherrees: "I went a few times when it was squatted. I can remember helping an American guy in the kitchen who decided to make chips for everyone and I was shocked he didn't know how to make them.

I was often there with my ear piercing gun and I remember Gabby with her hair clippers and a guy running off with just half a mohican cut.

There was a bucket for donations and some people would put just a few coppers in. I didn't know these back stories about the stabbing though."

Small Wonder

Small Wonder Records (1975-1983) was a small independent record label and shop that specialised in punk rock. It was based at 162 Hoe Street in Walthamstow in East London and was run by married couple Pete and Mari Stennett. Pete was quite a feisty character and some of his customer care stories are legend.

Leon AOH: "We all lived in the Leytonstone area of East London and had all got into punk together in 1978 .Pretty soon (in 79 I think) we discovered Small Wonder Record Shop in Walthamstow which was just a short bus ride from where we lived. It was fantastic to be so close to what was probably the best shop for punk and alternative music to have ever existed. I remember the excitement of our first visit ,peering through the shop window to ogle such an incredible array of records .They had everything from Crass to The Clash to The Cravats to The Cockney Rejects and even some bands whose name did not begin with the letter C. It took us a while to pluck up enough courage to enter the shop as the vibe emanating from it was paradoxically both incredibly alluring and infinitely intimidating .

Over time we became regular customers ,often bearing the brunt of Pete Stennets ,(Small Wonder's owner) sardonic humour as he gently joshed us about our sartorial and musical choices .I remember visiting the shop one day with our mate Deffy. He was very tall and skinny and dressed from head to toe in leopard skin print clothing with chains dangling from his body .Pete Stennet popped his head up over the counter,took one look at Deffy and called him "a long, lanky streak of bat's piss".

Small Wonder released several important and influential records by artists like The Cure, Angelic Upstarts, Cockney Rejects and Bauhaus. However perhaps the one record that broke the mould was The Feeding of the 5000 by Crass.

Recorded on the 29th of October 1978 by John Loder at Southern Studios in Wood Green after the band came to the attention of Pete at Small Wonder, its impact was immediate and far reaching, influencing a new generation of bands willing to take up the fight. Recorded as an 18 track 12" 45 rpm EP it proved to be a bit of a hot potato with workers at a record pressing plant in Ireland refusing to handle it due to the controversial irreligious nature of opening track "Asylum".

The record (Weeny 2) was eventually released with the offending track replaced by two minutes silence called "The Sound of Free Speech". This proved a turning point for the band which saw them setting up their own record label giving them carte blanche. "Reality Asylum" was released shortly afterwards in 1979 on Crass Records. It also took any heat off Pete and Small Wonder.

Pete did however release other records by other anarcho-punk artists like The Cravats "The End" 7" EP (Small Fifteen), "Precinct" / "Who's In Here With Me?" 7" (Small Twenty-Four), "You're Driving Me" / "I Am The Dreg" 7" (Small Twenty-Five), "Off The Beach" / "And The Sun Shone" 7" (Small Twenty-Six) and Cravats In Toytown LP (Cravat-1), Anthrax "You've Got It All Wrong" 7" EP (Small Twenty-Seven) and Poison Girls "Hex" 12" (Weeny Four) as well as the Fatal Microbes/Poison Girls "Beautiful Pictures" 12" (Weeny Three).

"The Tribe"

28a Leicester Square aka The Subway aka 'The Tribe' was a basement space that for a short time featured live performances every Tuesday by the likes of Blood and Roses (15/02/83 and 08/03/83), Brigandage (22/02/83 and 08/03/83), Action Pact + Wet Paint Theatre (12/04/83 and Hagar The Womb + Twisted Nerve (03/05/83).

Michael Moorcock's tv show 'South of Watford' did a programme long investigation in to 'Positive Punk' 18/03/83 shining a spotlight on The Tribe and the new punk and featured live music from Blood and Roses and Brigandage 08/03/83 as well as interviews with Jez James and Bob Short from Blood and Roses and Michelle Archer and Richard Cabut aka Richard North from Brigandage (at 39 Westbere Road aka Puppy Mansions 2). Michelle and Richard are filmed talking about their introduction to punk while Bob and Jez talk about what punk means to them and "the politics of the individual".

I spoke to Michelle about her memories of The Tribe and South of Watford. Michelle: "I don't remember much about the Tribe. It kinda merges into memories of the Batcave and Pigeon Toed Orange Peel clubs but I seem to remember a woman called Claudia had something to do with it... I'll always remember Claudia as she saved the night of the cancelled Scala all nighter debacle by inviting loads of us back to hers for a party after we all turned up to play ! The only reason I have any memories of The Tribe at all was that the shitshow South of Watford was filmed there. Agreeing to do that programme was one of the biggest mistakes I've ever made. They came and filmed us and Blood & Roses playing. After they interviewed us as a band . Some question came up about Nukes and some of the band were against; I mean I was too but I argued that at least Nukes MAD meant rich people's lives were in jeopardy as well as just the usual poor being sent to the trenches as cannon fodder.... I mention this as an example of the interview that we did apres show and was later cut out for footage of Stumpy the 3 legged cat at Puppy Mansions. This is where the real horror story starts not least because I decided to change a dress habit of a lifetime and not wear my usual androgynous bondage trousers and tee but instead wore a white mini dress with black tights and boots! Omfg! Video puts on 10lbs and lesson learnt never ever wear black tights with white dress! We were then plied with rocket fuel amphetamine which I wasn't going to complain about but jeezus we were gurning for England and I'd told my mum to watch! Look Ma I'm on top of the World and off my tits! Then after hours of footage discussing important stuff they chose the hairdryer bit as we got ready for filming.

In fact dearest Michael Moorcook, who interviewed us sent me a lovely letter hoping we weren't too disappointed in how the programme came out which was a bit of an understatement. That although the camera crew just kept asking when they were going to film the skinheads, the rest of film crew actually liked us and thought we were a good band yet still they took all the content out.

The rest of the band had a watch party only to see they had been sidelined for Richard's hair styling and me. Nothing was said but looking back resentment had begun to rear its ugly head and a suspicion that I had had something to do with them being cut out.

Although I was never given a reason as to why I was unceremoniously booted out the band I'd started I think this programme nightmare was the bit where the circle was broken and the magic destroyed. Our initial mistake was to turn down a record deal with Anagram; later with another record deal I refused to record a Thin Lizzy track as a B side then finally this total erasure from the Documentary. . I have never watched it since so I don't really remember what was in it. It was so hideously horrifying and distressing on so many levels I have tried to blank it from my mind. . . When I was thrown out of Brigandage my heart broke and it never recovered even though I stood up and started all over again I still feel that pain everyday."

Black Sheep Housing Co-op

109 Corbyn Street

According to Puppy Alistair Livingstone the original inspiration for the Alternative Housing Co-op (or as it became known the Black Sheep Housing Co-op) came from Andy Martin of The Apostles.

Black Sheep offered a better, more secure way of living for those involved. A "PUNKS' PARADISE" if you will. So screamed an indignant headline in The Standard when in 1983 Islington Council handed over four properties - 109 Corbyn Street, 103 Grosvenor Avenue and 53 and 59 Cross Street, that had fallen in to disrepair, to Black Sheep Housing Co-op on a short-term lease.

109 Corbyn Street was once the home of local artist Richard Crow aka Scarecrow who lived and worked there from 1983 until 2008. The space was called the Institution of Rot which he co-founded with Nick Couldry in 1993. Richard was also a member of the Scum Collective and had previously been a member of musical group The Turdburglers (alongside Luggy Lugworm and Mark Ripper) and Hagar The Womb. He was The Hags first drummer. He shared the house with his then girlfriend Anna Scheer and Maria Burton. Anna ran the Southern Death Cult fan club. Maria photographed The Cult in Richard's art space for ZigZag in either 1984 or 1985. The front door still has a handle that was fixed to it by Maria's then significant other Dominic Brown.

103 Grosvenor Avenue

The masonry work (painted by Richard) still looks as it did then.

Mark Mob helped renovate houses for the Co-op with All The Madmen setting down roots at 103 Grosvenor Avenue (three floors and a garden and the first property to be leased to Black Sheep) before moving to Brougham Road two years later in 1985. Jeremy Gluck, who would find fame and fortune with The Barracudas and who was a member of the Puppy collective, also lent a hand with the renovation work as did Pip (Smith). Here's Al Puppy again: "Nearly all the work done to convert four derelict houses to a liveable standard was done 'in house'. We had

53 Cross Street　　　　　　　　*Original wall covering*

gas-fitters and roofers, joiners, plumbers, electricians, painters... all the skills needed found amongst anarcho-punk-goth community. Maybe the NME sub-editor should have called us "Practical Punks"." Mark Mob aka Mark Wilson designed the Black Sheep Housing Co-op stamp.

Mark + Min and Al Puppy spent an evening on the 2nd of September holed up at 103 stuffing 500 copies of Witch Hunt in to their sleeves... And it was at 103 that Tony Drayton wrote the very last issue of Kill Your Pet Puppy.

Mark bought a truck and made himself a tipi over the winter of 1983/84 whilst living at 103 Grosvenor Avenue.

Fod, Mick Lugworm and Sarah Washington (then Fod's partner) also lived at 103. Sarah was a big Psychic TV fan and would baby sit for Gen and Paula.

In January 1984 at a party at 103 Grosvenor Avenue Al Puppy met his future partner Pinki aka Rebecca Livingstone aka Tanith. Pinki was extremely active in protesting the deployment of Cruise missiles on

50 Beck Road. Once home to Genesis P-Orridge, wife Paula and their two daughters Caresse and Genesse.

British soil and became a familiar face at Greenham Common where she lived between 1981 and 1984. She even featured in Beeban Kidron and Amanda Richardson's documentary Carry Greenham Home (1983). Pinki also played a crucial role in organising Stop The City with anarchist postman and future McLibel defendant Dave Morris. Pinki passed away on the 5th of January 1996. She was just 33.

53 Cross Street has an extraordinary history made famous by art lecturer Martin King who moved in in 1989. The five-storey Georgian property which was built in 1785 held many secrets to its past. Hidden beneath floorboards and behind loose walls were treasures aplenty. Martin and housemate Mark McAuley discovered 19th-century ink bottles, bits of brass, a 19th-century iron, and fragments of pots and clay pipes. They uncovered an old scullery and an original fireplace. They even discovered hidden beneath the floor walnut shells whose age was determined to be approximately 200 years old. Martin set about writing a book - "53 Cross Street: The Biography of a House", published by Islington Archaeology & History Society in 2007. It retails at £21. However Islington council put

59 Cross Street

the house up for sale in 2003. It was sold to a developer for a tidy sum – £600,000, who sold it on to a businessman.

Moving on. 59 Cross Street's most famous occupant was Andy Palmer who moved in after leaving Crass and Dial House. Some of his fellow residents included Andy Barker aka Andy Stratton of Null & Void fame, Gem Stone (Rubella Ballet) and Lou aka Louise Challice (Hysteria Ward).

154 New North Road

A veritable who's who lived there including Mark Mob, Mark's younger brother Paul, Greenhair, Debbie (My Bloody Valentine), Val Drayton, Richard Cabut aka Richard North (who took his name from the New North Road property), Tom Vague, Al Puppy, Anna Scheer (Scarecrow's girlfriend), Maria Burton and Ian Astbury and his then girlfriend

Jacqueline Mathers. Jacqueline is descended from British occult royalty, Samuel Liddell Mathers, who in 1887 co-founded the Hermetic Order of the Golden Dawn.

Ian Astbury is best known for his involvement in a trio of bands – Southern Death Cult, Death Cult and The Cult. What is perhaps not known is his involvement in the anarcho-punk scene. In 1980 as a young man he shadowed Crass and Poison Girls on the Northern Tour on October 7th-19th. He was a regular at Dial House and it was on one such visit that he was given a copy of Black Elk Speaks by Eve. The book left quite an impression on Ian. Sid Ation (Rubella Ballet) says that Ian was a frequent visitor to the Poison Girls house in Leytonstone, often popping round for a cuppa and a chat. Sid met up with Ian again when Rubella joined Death Cult on tour across the UK in September of 1983.

Anna and Marie wrote an article "Magik and Greenham Common" for Vague.

I took a moment to speak to Tom Vague about his recollections of living at 154. Tom:

"The Vague fanzine office moved to 154 New North Road in Islington in 1983 as our west country neighbours the Mob moved out to Grosvenor Avenue, when they formed the Black Sheep housing co-op. At this time the Vague editorial staff included Anna Scheer and Maria Burton, the Southern Death Cult merchandiser muses, as the positive-punk group was splitting up and the singer Ian Astbury was teaming up with Billy Duffy from Theatre of Hate as Death Cult-The Cult. I think this largely took place at 154 New North Road as Ian took over my old room in the damp basement with his girlfriend Jacqueline Mathers, a descendant/great-granddaughter? of the co-founder of the Order of the Golden Dawn Samuel Liddell Mathers. Jacqueline was a really down-to-earth beautiful Bradford lass but once scared the shit out of me when she grabbed my bum at the bar in Heaven; and I was nicked with her bunking the tube to Brixton to visit Billy but we were let off due to her occult powers.

At first we were sharing 154 with Les of V-sign fanzine and his girlfriend from the Mob and Blood and Roses scene. I introduced Ian Astbury to Mark Mob outside 154 on New North Road and they seemed to get on OK although Ian was moving away from his anarcho-punk roots at the time.

We ended up sharing the house with the Amebix from Bristol after Welsh Sam(antha) Railton moved them into the room next to mine. I relocated with them to the Anarchy Centre on Roseberry Avenue when we were duly evicted from 154 in late 1983. A few of Xmal Deutschland also stayed there when I was doing their tour merchandising.

I went to see 'Monty Python's The Meaning of Life' from 154 with Ian Astbury and Jacqueline Mathers. Ian really pissed off the next door neighbours throwing bits of the banisters into the back garden before we were evicted, and he did some great anti-Goth graffiti art in the living room. Billy Duffy didn't convert me to Led Zeppelin at New North Road but I've since come round to that occult Cult influence."

April Housing Co-op

109 Foulden Road

April Housing Co-op owned three properties in Stoke Newington.

First of all 109 Foulden Road. Once the humble abode of Andy Martin. A "squadron of militant lesbians... occupied the first three floors". Andy stayed in the attic which played host to several bands who took advantage of Andy's hospitality. The Snails (who Andy joined on lead guitar) rehearsed there "on a 1960s drum kit and amplifiers provided by Pete, Julian and Dan of The Apostles" as did Flack (whose line-up included Mitch from the Hags who stepped in to fill the shoes of Martha Moscow on bass). Snails guitar player Paul Van-Transit would later go on to join This Bitter Lesson (who released two cassettes - Value of Defiance and This Bitter Lesson courtesy of 96 Tapes in 1982) and Faction. During this period (February 1982) Andy also played guitar for Faction whose first demo was recorded in Andy's attic.

Lou (Louise Challice) moved in. Lou and Andy got on like a house on fire and even recorded several songs there together. It was on one of her commutes to Stoke Newington that she first met Rob Challice.

Andy (Co-op Secretary) who perhaps due to his association with Faction and Blood and Roses, played his part in Fod and Marti Cosmos aka Martin Cobb (Faction) and Bob and Lisa and Richard Morgan joining the April Housing Co-op.

Then it was 44 Bayston Road's turn. Those who set up home there

44 Bayston Road

included Scarecrow, Cristina Mazzoni, Fod, Bob, Ann Gee Zoff and Mouse.

And finally 32a Yoakley Road. The toilet and the "pyramid of poo" became the stuff of legend. Bob (Short) was the only one brave enough to venture in to the lavatory. Hackney council had to remove 90 bin bags of human faeces from the garden. Those residing in its resplendent surroundings included Bob and his girlfriend Ann Gee Zoff, Cristina, Scarecrow, Martin Cobb, Matt and Jacob MacLeod and Fod. Matt and Jacob have a famous father and mother - Manfred Mann's lead singer Paul Jones and Scottish feminist and author Sheila Macleod. Fod was a member of the "Kent contingent" who like Rob Challice had also accrued some time in Anthrax before relocating to London. Fod turned his artistic skills to designing the sleeve for Blood and Roses' first 12" EP 'Love

32a Yoakley Road

Under Will'. The design was "based a lot on Tarot trumps and iconography from reading Kenneth Grants 'Outside The Circles of Time'." Both Rob and Fod (and Oskar aka Gary Budd from Anthrax) were editors of Enigma fanzine which featured contributions from Scarecrow, Ann Dee Martian aka Andy Martin, Mark F aka Mark Ferelli (Part 1) and Matt MacLeod. Matt and Jake and Scarecrow and Fod were also involved with The Apostles (Ann Dee Martian, Pete Byng-Hall and Julian Portinari) fanzine Scum.

One terrifying cold winter evening 32a was attacked by skinheads who broke in and smashed all the windows. Bob barricaded himself in, Fod leapt from a upstairs window and Black Luke was thrown from an upstairs window in to the front garden.

Cazenove Road + 2 Glading Terrace
and 1 Batley Road

57 Cazenove Road

58 Cazenove Road

Let's look at some other squatted properties in Stoke Newington.

Cazenove Road. Stu Jellyfish and Jez James (Blood and Roses) stayed upstairs at number 57. Chris Sparks (Managing Directors) and girlfriend Helen lived downstairs. Min Kent (Zos Kia) and Phil Ritchie lived opposite at 58 Cazenove Road. Min had previously stayed in a shared house - 51 Huntingdon Street with Phil, Jellyfish, Cory and Pip before eventually moving to Beck Road and Psychic TV HQ en route by way of 103 Grosvenor Avenue.

2 Glading Terrace. Andy Martin and Sniper (The Heretics and Black Cross with Angie Wynn aka Ann Gee Zoff, Scarecrow, and Andy) stayed in this housing co-op property. Bad Manners' Buster Bloodvessel lived in a flat downstairs. Swell Map and Television Personality Jowe Head also lived on Glading Terrace.

1 Batley Road. Phil Ritchie, Bob Short + Lisa Kirby, Leah Durkan (who stayed in the front ground floor room) and Sack (Cobalt Hate fanzine) lived here.

2 Glading Terrace

1 Batley Road

Cobalt Hate was a no nonsense fanzine from Stevenage. On the 14th December 1979 Crass, Poison Girls and UK Decay (who were then part of a Luton based fanzine collective) played a benefit raising funds for Cobalt Hate #3 in an old World War 2 Nissen Hut next to Marsh Farm Community Centre, Luton. 250 enthusiastic punks squeezed in to the small military shelter. Afterwards UK Decay, Crass and Poison Girls became fast friends. Bernhardt Rebours (Poison Girls) designed sleeves for a trilogy of releases by UK Decay including Sexual (FRESH 33), For Madmen Only (FRESH LP5/A) and Rising From The Dread (Christ ITS 1).

Puppy Mansions 1 & 2

Puppy Mansions 1 at 33 Sheriff Road. Tony Drayton aka Tony D first encountered Kevin Mooney (who would become familiar to all of us as a future Ant) at one of the upstairs windows. Adam Ant's ex-wife Eve also lived there. One of the regular visitors to the house was Mark Moore (then a schoolboy) who'd turn up with Ants bootlegs. Mark would go on to find success as a DJ and a record producer topping the charts with S'Xpress.

The house was run by the West Hampstead Housing Association. And it's where fanzine Kill Your Pet Puppy was first conceived in December 1979. Housemates Val (Drayton) and Brett and Sex Gang Child Dave Roberts were also involved as was Jeremy Gluck who would go on to find fame and fortune with The Barracudas who's single "Summer Fun" reached number 37 in the UK singles charts in 1980.

They would become known as the Puppy Collective. Before that Tony had published the glorious Ripped and Torn 1976-1979, the go to zine for all things punk. KYPP was called Fuck Your Mother until Andy Palmer dissuaded Tony after a phone call to Dial House. Joly MacFie from Better Badges would cover any printing costs and handle distribution after a deal was struck with Tony. KYPP1 was born. Brett Puppy drew the logo (and cover). 500 copies flew out the door at the Adam and the Ants show at the Electric Ballroom, January 1st 1980. Issue number 2 came out in February of that year.

Puppy Mansions 1

Tony D outside Puppy Mansions 1

Puppy Mansions 2   *Tony D outside Puppy Mansions 2*

The collective moved to new premises after another West Hampstead Housing Association property became available at 39 Westbere Road. Puppy Mansions 2! Hags Elaine, Karen and Ruth lived here as did Louise Harris aka Louise Callice (Hysteria Ward and The Witches with Ann Gee Zoff) and Mick Lugworm.

Four more issues would follow, the last of which (number 6) would eventually be published in 1984. Issues 4 and 5 were printed by Little 'A' Printers.

Various puppies sat for talented artist and neighbour Jo Brocklehurst (1935-2006). Brocklehurst dedicated her life to documenting the extraordinary and the fabulous. "The streets are full of marvelous people, you've only got to look." she said. Fashion was her passion. She visited London's fetish clubs and Berlin's clubland and art houses. But it was her drawings of the anarcho-punks of 39 Westbere Road in all their flamboyant splendour that really captured the imagination. Jo lived at number 12 until her death in 2006.

Tony recalls when Philip Salon (who is perhaps best remembered for his part in the Bromley Contingent and who coincidentally ran 'The Mud Club' where Mark Moore got his start as a DJ) and Boy George came to visit.

Spanish Lisa, the star of The Stranglers "Strange Little Girl" video, was a frequent visitor to Puppy Mansions 2. Elaine Reubens from the Hags also appears in the video. Elaine: "We got paid a tenner each and the main girl got £100 as she agreed to have her head shaved; the rest of us wimped out. We were also fed and spent a merry ten minutes pelting buns at a Sun photographer who ran and hid in a phone box. Whilst we continued to bombard him with bread products.

My main memory – was of a group of us running up and down and shouting Jean Jacques at the top of our voices in cod French accents. We were very young and it made us laugh till we all got sore sides and hiccups."

Ruth (Elias) drew the giraffe from the cover of Hagar The Womb's 12" 'The Word of the Womb' on Mortarhate (MORT2 in 1984) on her bedroom wall there.

The house features in Michael Moorcock's 'South of Watford' tv show on positive punk dated March 18th 1983 following the publication of Richard North's piece for the NME called 'Punk Warriors', 19th February 1983. Richard and Michelle Brigandage are filmed talking about their introduction to punk. We also get a glimpse of Michelle blow drying Richard's hair while talking about Chris Ward and Wet Paint Theatre Company of which she was a member. In 1985 Michelle appeared in a revival of Chris' 1983 play Amphibious Babies where she plays Burgundy, stepping in to the shoes of Ruth Radish (from Hagar the Womb) who played the exact same role during the play's first theatrical run.

Wet Paint Theatre Company and The Metropolitan Theatre

Wet Paint Theatre Company "The world's ONLY punk theatre" was founded in 1981 by writer/director Chris Ward. It dared to tread where other theatre companies did not, introducing theatre to a non-theatre going audience, for example performing alongside rock acts of the day. Breaking down barriers if you will. Chris would also have members of said bands take on major roles in many of his most memorable theatre productions. "Yer, well it's like that... you could probably get like these RSC actresses spouting off their lines and that - but it's all so phoney. When you've got people doing it like this it's the truth out there because they really believe what they're saying."

In January 1982 the company played two dates (29/01/82 and 30/01/82) at the Windmill Theatre, Great Windmill Street, London W1 with the UK Subs.

On Monday September 20th and 27th WP appeared (alongside Conflict, Rubella Ballet, Omega Tribe and Poison Girls) at a mini festival "Nights To Slash Your Wrists By!!" at The Grove Theatre, Hammersmith W6. "£1 if you've slashed your wrists! OR £1.50 if you haven't."

In 1984 Conflict, Reality, Decadent Few, Hagar The Womb, Subhumans, Karma Sutra, Lost Cherrees, The Sears, Vex, Exit-Stance, Flowers in the Dustbin, Icons of Filth, Tom's Midnight Garden, Legion of Parasites, The Committee and Splattered Afterbirth would appear on a shared bill next to Wet Paint at "What's All This Let's Be Liberal And Tolerate 'Em Shit", a festival which ran from the 7th until the 20th of August at the Metropolitan Theatre Pub, 95 Farringdon Road, London EC1. It was organised by Colin Conflict in conjunction with Wet Paint Theatre Company. Bands performed every night between 8pm and 11pm. Wet Paint performed Chris Ward's 1984 play "Cat Food" which premiered at the Metropolitan, June 5th 1984. It did so to much acclaim.

On the 2nd of March 1985 16 Guns and Carnage joined Wet Paint at The Three Johns in Islington N1. 16 Guns guitar player Paul Lyne took up with WPT following his departure from the band. Paul passed away in 2019.

Things got lairy when things took a violent twist when they performed at the Blue Coat Boy (Skunx) to "hostile neo-Nazi audiences". Skunx had an unsavoury reputation. It was run by Syndicate Records supremo Dave Long. Long also managed Splodgenessabounds and Croydon Oisters Case. Oi! the Club if you will. According to Ian Glasper Anthrax played there on Saturday the 26th of March 1982 (with X-Cretas and Lost Cherrees) and narrowly escaped with their lives. Singer Gary recalls someone running through the bar whilst brandishing an axe. The Subhumans, Organised Chaos and Assassins of Hope also played at this rather inauspicious venue on April 3rd 1982.

Other Wet Paint productions included "Demonstration of Affection" (at London's Experimental Arts Theatre starring Honey Bane and Richard Jobson from The Skids which proved somewhat of a prickly topic due to its sultry "live sex" scenes involving its stars. "The sex is for real, it's not faked." said Honey Bane in a retort and "love the energy, pity I couldn't keep up the pace!" commented Minor Threat frontman Ian MacKaye.), Plastic Zion"(starring Beki Bondage and George Cheex from Action Pact), "Amphibious Babies" (starring Michelle Brigandage and Ruth Elias aka Ruth Radish) and "Camberwell Beauty" (with Max Splodge). "Colourful Hagar the Womb vocalist Ruth Radish is a revelation" says Sounds journo Johnny Waller February 19, 1984.

It was reported in music weekly Sounds that Colin Conflict would take on an acting role opposite Beki Bondage in Camberwell Beauty. Sadly this never came to pass.

I spoke to Dev (Tom's Midnight Garden) about some of his recollections. Dev: "We're all on a journey up and down the tree of life, and during that journey there are many day trips; a branch here, a branch there; you get off the boat, sometimes it's a walk, sometimes a jungle, sometimes a fucking mountain, but it's all experience and growth, filled with up's n downs n turnarounds (cheers Barney) and if you're unlucky, you eventually grow up. In 1984, I was 16 years old and on one of them "day trips"... OK, enough of the poncey metaphors, I'll try and get to the point... What is the point? Well, David has asked me to write a bit about the short time over the summer of '84 that The Metropolitan Tavern (situated on the junction of Farringdon Rd and Clerkenwell Rd in London EC1) was a hang-out for punks. But to write about that, I've gotta write about the Wet Paint Theatre, so buckle up and let me rewind a bit. By 1983, I'd been in a couple of bands but got bored of playing Oi!/Real Punk music and wanted to try something a bit different. There was a buzz around a new bunch of bands that, for arguments sake, were influenced more by Joy Division than Sham, and at around the same time, at a mate's gig, I'd seen a play by Wet Paint Theatre, fundamentally, a "punk" theatre company centred around a writer named Chris Ward with his actor friends and a revolving door of punky celeb's, such as Beki Bondage and Michelle Brigandage. Well, I thought all this was quite sophisticated, lumped it all together, grew a trendy Mohican and started my own new band TMG (Tom's Midnight Garden). Sadly, that post punk moment of aspiration lost inspiration and very quickly got rinsed out amongst a load of sub-blitz kid hype in the music press, but that's another story. Most of the bands split, but it didn't stop Wet Paint, who appeared on the front cover of Time Out and forged a few more inroads with contemporary venues and contacts, such as The Scala, Kathy Acker and Nick Cave. Some way through 1984, in a seemingly sideways move, they secured a summer-long residency at The Metropolitan to showcase their play 'Cat Food' while simultaneously providing a platform for many young street level punk groups to bang out a set. Yeah, you guessed it, TMG were one such band and we played there on three occasions. The pub itself was a fairly typical '80s boozer; like a lot of City pubs, lunchtimes were busy with folk who worked nearby, while evening doors were generally quieter with a few locals and the odd shift worker, so the landlord would have been happy with the extra trade we brought in on typically dead Monday evenings. I don't remember the pub being that big, you'd walk in and there was a central bar, I used to sit at a table to the left by the front window which had easy access to the old, creaky staircase that led to the basement where all the festivities took place. It was dark 'n' dingey with a small stage at the back left hand corner where a Wet Paint Theatre backdrop was mounted with gaffer tape. Alcohol was integral to proceedings, but there was no bar down there, so appetites were appeased by staggered trips upstairs and good old-fashioned lager and cider smuggling. I'd say there was just enough space down there for about 100 of us reprobates, there was no window, air-con or fan... it was hot and stank of sweat and spilt beer... it was great.

The Metropolitan had a similar vibe to the larger 'Burn It Down Ballroom' but without the chaos... certainly, each time I was at the place there was a great atmosphere; one big party, never any trouble, lots of laughing, dancing and drinking and that's no mean feat as there was still quite a bit of bother at gigs in those days... maybe The Metropolitan was one of punks best kept secrets, hahaha. Initially events attracted a fairly balanced crowd from the (then) large squatting community and the wider punk scene, and 40 years later, I can still remember many familiar faces in attendance. The first time we played, Marc Almond (Soft Cell/Mambas) was outside debating whether to come in and witness us murder 'Tainted Love', a song we were known for playing; however, towards the end of the summer it seemed to have become more dominated by "Anarcho" types, a punk subdivision which, despite my love for early Crass, I had very little to do with. Wet Paint may have been, and still be "anarchic" but I'd imagine they weren't particularly excited about being restricted to any one label, let alone one that was often, but not always, the domain of rich kids taking a year out of the system before going to university and becoming part of it. It was a pigeon-hole that played a significant part in my decision to leave TMG after just nine glorious gig-packed months. It was ironic yet perfectly fitting that we played our last gig at The Metropolitan. This day trip was over for me; I shaved my head again and started a new band with a new sound.

A few weeks later, at the end of August, Wet Paint packed up their bags and, in true travelling theatre company style, moved up the road to Camden, thus ending The Metropolitan Tavern's brief encounter with the London punk scene. Sadly, like so many of our old and historic drinking holes, the pub closed its doors in 1988 and was raised to the ground the following year.

Footnote: Other bands that played at The Metropolitan included: Decadent Few, Disease, Flowers In The Dustbin, Icons Of Filth, Reality, Brigandage, The Committee, Hagar The Womb, Karma Sutra, Lost Cherrees, Vex... "

Written by Dev (sowilomedia.net)

The Moonlight Club

The Railway, once home to The Moonlight Club (which was run by Dave Kitson from October 1979 until 1993) was Tony's local where he once met Ian Curtis on the evening of Joy Division's final live performance May 2nd 1980. Ian died in Macclesfield just two weeks later on the 18th of May.

The residents of number 33 Sherriff Road could often be found at The Railway supping pints while enjoying various musical delights on stage. Crass played there (25/10/1978) as they did on March 7th and 8th at a benefit for International Anthem with The Epileptics and Poison Girls, UK Decay did so on the 28th of January 1980, The Cravats (05/01/81), Zounds and Flux of Pink Indians (03/12/80), Zounds and The Room (10/09/81), Poison Girls and Rubella Ballet (28/09/81), Zounds and Parting Shots (20/10/81), Zounds and Parting Shots (20/10/81), Conflict, Rubella Ballet and Anthrax (20/01/82), Southern Death Cult (18/08/82), DIRT and Flux of Pink Indians (19/08/82), Flux of Pink Indians and Faction (23rd August 1982), The Sinyx, Riot/Clone and Rudimentary Peni (11/09/82), Conflict, Anthrax, Hagar The Womb and The Sears (on the 26th of September 1982), Blood and Roses, Cold War and Twelve Cubic Feet (November 10th 1982), Flowers In The Dustbin (15th February

1984), Subhumans, Rubella Ballet and Evil Eye (18/04/84). Zillah Minx: "We decided to hire and promote our own gig after seeing CRASS play there and Gee told us "you can hire this place for free and put on your own gigs". So we did."

The Subhumans/Faction recordings were released on cassette courtesy of Bluurg and 96 Tapes.

Street-Level + Fuck Off Records

Fuck Off Records & Tapes

The 'idiot's picnics' (at Meanwhile Gardens 1977-1988) featuring the talents of artists like The Astronauts, Blyth Power, The Mob, Omega Tribe and Androids of Mu, were the work of Lancaster Music Co-op and Grant Showbiz.

Showbiz aka Grant Cunliffe had cut his teeth as a sound man working with Here & Now and on the free festival circuit as an MC. From there he carved out a career as a producer, working with the likes of The Fall, The Mob, The Astronauts, Blue Midnight (a band which he founded with Dave Johnson), The Instant Automatons (Protag and Mark Lancaster) and Mark P's The Good Missionaries.

His base of operations was Street-Level Studios, the next stop on our journey at 8 Bristol Gardens, which he set up with Kif Kif aka Keith Dobson and José Gross from Here & Now in 1979.

In 1980 Six Minute War's debut 7 "More Short Songs" was recorded at Street Level Studios and engineered by Kif Kif. One reviewer described it thus: " The follow up to the widely acclaimed and popular debut maxi-EP, this is more of the same. Another 6 Crass/early ATV type songs about wars, government, youth labels. selling out and the token joke track. If you like this sort of stuff then buy it - I do and I did.(At only 50p it's a better buy than the new Toxic Graffity with its average Crass freebie)." From Kill Your Pet Puppy #3 1980.

Pete Fender - Four Formulas (For The Eradication Of Microbes) XN 2002 was recorded at Street Level on 17th, 29th and 30th September 1980. Production was by Richard Famous and Pete Fender. Artwork by Bernhardt Rebours.

In 1985 Blyth Power recorded the Chevy Chase 7" (MAD 9) at Street Level December 1st 1985.

Next stop 235 Lancaster Road (1 and 2 Whitchurch Road) once home to Fuck Off Records and Tapes (and Lancaster Housing and Music Project). Founded in 1979 by Here & Now roadie Jonathan Barnett and Kif Kif after The Instant Automatons cassette Radio Silence: Art of Human Error inspired them to set up their own cassette label. Using Here & Now's business model they were up and running.

One of Fuck Off's most celebrated releases was Blood Robots by Androids of Mu. (FLP001) Released in 1980 and featuring Suze Da Blooze from Here And Now on vocals it wowed fans and critics alike.

In 1984 FO released the "FYM" cassette (FO1001) by Brigandage.

FO had then moved to new premises from 286 Portobello Road to 97 Caledonian Road where they also shared a space with Better Badges and All The Madmen.

Which brings us to the Weird Tales Tour and Weird Tales Tapes. The Mob, The Astronauts, Zounds, Androids of Mu and Bob Green began wowing audiences around the country.

In 1982 Weird Tales Tapes released a compilation cassette "A Tribute To Bert Weeden" which included various demos recorded at Street Level sessions by Zounds (A1–8), The Mob (A9–B3) and Androids of Mu (B5–B10).

51 Huntingdon Street

Min, Cory, Pip, Jellyfish, Slack (Cobalt Hate), Angela Blowjob, Scottish Jimmy and Phil were amongst some of those ensconced at number 51 or H. Street, a former corner shop with its windows shored up by breeze blocks.

Phil: "Huntingdon St was a real golden era for me. Things started to feel more safer than the days of Campbell Buildings the glue and tuinol were replaced with the return of speed and lots of acid and I started to explore my/our politics in a lot more depth."

Phil again: "It was a paradise compared to what me, Cory, Pip & Evelyn had moved from! (Campbell Buildings) And we did have the front door wired to the mains electricity to give the skins a nasty shock!" The local NF would come round and say that they were going to firebomb the property.

Philip Salon, Boy George and Mark Moore were amongst some of its celebrity visitors.

Pip put pen to paper and wrote a "gay punks" article for Gay Noise magazine. Entitled "Gay Punx = Bent or Yer Arse Is 'Anging Owt!" it was published on October 23rd 1980 in issue No 6. This proved pivotal. Two scenes coalesced. In 1981 Pip invited the Puppy Collective over for a meal. A galvanising moment if you will.

And there was the leopard print wall painted by Pip and Jellyfish.

Anarchy magazine and 29 Grosvenor Avenue

29 Grosvenor Avenue was a four-storey-squatted property in Newington Green N16. From 1972 until 1985 it was home to Anarchy magazine which was produced under the watchful gaze of Charlotte Baggins, her partner Chris Broad and Phil Ruff.

The Second Series (Series 1 was produced by Freedom Press from March 1961 until December 1970 under the tutelage of Colin Ward) saw the publication strike out on its own.

In 1972 Anarchy moved to Grosvenor Avenue. A commune of sorts attracting activists of various hues and colours it was raided by the Bomb

Squad and Special Branch amassing evidence against Jake Prescott, Ian Purdie and the Stoke Newington Eight.

After a stroke of good fortune Chris Broad purchased a printing press for the purposes of printing Anarchy. He and Charlotte transformed the printing operation in the basement of number 29 in to Little 'A' Printers. Martin Wright, Dave Morris, Dave Coul and Stoke Newington Eight defendant Kate McLean were amongst some of those who joined the collective during this period. When the council took back the property Chris and Charlotte moved out and Little 'A' found a new home at Metropolitan Wharf in Wapping.

"The press was equipped with decrepit Multiliths, Rotaprint R20s and R30s, and the rent was 50p /sq ft (the founders had to scrape molasses off the floor and walls, put up drywall, install running water and sanitation.) We used to eat our chips on a loading platform right over the swirling brown water of the Thames."

In 1978 the Anarchy Collective folded. In 1982 it got a new lick of paint under the editorial leadership of Phil Ruff, Vince Stevenson (Rising Free) and Robyn Miles (Anarchist Black Cross). Iris Mills, Ronan Bennett and Stuart Christie also lent a hand. Issue #34 in 1982 featured interviews with Crass and Poison Girls.

In 1985 the Anarchy Collective dissolved for good.

Rising Free and 182 Upper Street

Rising Free anarchist bookshop formerly of 197 Kings Cross Road 1974–1981 moved to 182 Upper Street but a stone's throw from Molly's. Rising Free was open six days a week 10.30–6.00.

Its stock was famously replenished in true anarchist style by books that had been nicked from other book shops.

Welsh anarchist Dafydd Ladd (a Persons Unknown co-conspirator who jumped bail and went on the run and who wrote for Zero, a London-based anarchist/anarcha-feminist monthly magazine in the 1970s) was a member of the Rising Free collective as was his fellow co-conspirator Vince Stevenson.

The London Workers Group was a "diverse collective of council communists, anarchist communists and anarcho-syndicalists." The group (founded by Dave Morris + Joe Thomas and Adam Flowers in 1977) met every fortnight at 'Rising Free'.

In the 1980s after the demise of Anarchy, LWG and the Workers' Playtime collective inherited Little 'A'. Workers Playtime which ran for 10 issues from February 1983 until May 1985 was a political journal produced by some members of LWG.

There were some discussions regarding cementing relations with other like minded groups for example with the Syndicalist Workers Federation (an early forerunner of the Direct Action Movement and Solidarity Federation) but these petered out. After LWG folded in 1985 some of its members went on to play a participatory role in the formation of Class War.

Rising Free even gave Nottingham radical bookseller Ross Bradshaw his start in Aberdeen in the 1970s.

Rising Free is now a jewellers.

The Pied Bull

The Pied Bull (1 Liverpool Road N1) was immortalised on Crass' second album Stations of the Crass released 1979 Cat. no 521984. Side Four was recorded live at Pied Bull, Islington, August 7, 1979.

The tracks are as follows:

- 21 System

- 22 Big Man, Big M.A.N.

- 23 Banned From The Roxy

- 24 Hurry Up Gary

- 25 Time Out

- 26 They've Got A Bomb

- 27 Fight War, Not Wars

- 28 Women

- 29 Shaved Women

- 30 You Pay

- 31 Heard Too Much About

- 32 Angels

- 33 What A Shame

- 34 So what

- 35 G's Song

- 36 Do They Owe Us A Living

- 37 Punk is Dead

On December 16th 1981 DIRT rolled up to play at this popular music venue followed by Conflict, Anthrax and Sinyx (February 20th 1982), Lack of Knowledge, Vertical Hold, Screaming Babies, Burnt Thighs and Dead Souls (March 8th 1982), Lost Cherrees (July 22nd 1982), Kronstadt Uprising (August 9th 1982), Hagar the Womb, Six Minute War, Youth In Asia and Assassins of Hope (September 3rd 1982), The Mob, Blood and Roses Null & Void and Universal Adhesion (September 28th 1982), Anthrax, X-Cretas and Fallout (November 22nd 1982), Subhumans and Destructors (February 14th 1983) and Brigandage, Play Dead and A Short Commercial Break (February 16th 1983).

It is now a building society.

Shoreditch Fire Station and Campbell Buildings

By the summer 1979 people had taken up residence in Shoreditch Fire Station, Tabernacle St EC2. Those who made it their home included Louise Challice, Jessica Jones, Val Drayton, Leigh Kendall, Brett Puppy,

Dave Sex Gang, Bob Short, Mitch, Gerry Ford, Ruthless aka Ruth Tyndall and a returning Tony D fresh from his latest adventure in Europe.

Built in 1895, station B27, the fire station was a five story building that enclosed a central courtyard. It stopped being an active fire station in 1964. The upper floors were decorated with pigeon droppings.

Lou had a room above Val and her friend Mitch aka Michelle. According to Val, Mitch was highly skilled at shoplifting - the best in the house. Bob stayed in the bell tower. On the ground floor was a car repair shop. The basement became a musicians playground where Lou remembers singing The Shangri-Las' Leader of the Pack accompanied by Bob on guitar. Bob and Ruthless decided to form a band with two other musicians Jock and Beano. Here's Bob: "A band in theory, yes. We could certainly wander the streets of London and claim to be in a band but we never played or rehearsed. Jock went off to join the bloody army which seemed a damn peculiar choice for a skinny Sid Vicious clone. Time passed and Ruth and I found ourselves washed ashore in Campbell Buildings SE1."

Val applied her hairdressing skills giving residents colourful hair treatments using assorted Crazy Colour hair dyes. Bob fed the house every Giro day returning home with catering size tins of baked beans.

On one rather dull Saturday afternoon and high on glue the idea was hatched to push a cooker from the fifth floor balcony much to the merriment of everyone who witnessed it.

By 1979 the skinhead threat had become very real and local BM skinheads led an attack on the fire station. However the skinhead threat did have its whimsical side. Val: "I remember one night at Old Street, sitting knitting one of my punk-rock holey jumpers in the 'living' room, when two skinheads climbed in through the (first floor) window, clearly with agro on their minds. Obviously expecting a heathen, punk horde, or at least some stealable equipment, they were competely taken aback to find just me, knitting. I ended up teaching them both how to knit! Very bizarre night. I think they became regular visitors after that..."

Finally when the threat of eviction loomed people fought tooth and nail to stay. They even went to the High Court. Sadly it was all to no avail and an eviction notice was served.

Some made a new home in an abandoned hospital in North West London - St Monica's Home for Sick Children, 16 Brondesbury Park, NW2 7BR 1874 - 1939 while others like Ruth, (Aussie) Bob and Mitch moved to Campbell Buildings, Waterloo - sprawling Victorian era flats (300) that gained some notoriety. Life on the estate was hard. Many of its occupants lived in absolute squalor. Del Blyben: "The place was filthy but Ruthless and Mitch had found ways to combat the pile up of rubbish by sweeping it into the corners and under the carpet.

Apart from the smell this worked fine for a while, until one fine sunny day when light found its way into the corners of the room as well. At first my eyes noticed but my brain didn't register that the carpet was moving all by itself in the sunlight. While my brain caught up Mitch noticed me staring at the gently undulating carpet in the corner of the room. She got up and beckoned me over then she pulled the carpet back to reveal a thick layer of maggots. There must have been thousands of them, but apparently they got rid of the rubbish so were left alone 'for the time being'."

Pinki and Lisa (Kirby) shared a room at Campbell Buildings.

Rockabillies tried to burn it down.

Local doctor "old moggy Manch"would liberally dish out pills. "I wouldn't feed these to a dog."

When the Old Bill popped round residents would hide their drugs in ceiling tiles.

In 1981 Crap aka Gary Critchley was convicted of the murder of Edward McNeil. McNeil had been beaten to death. Gary sustained serious injuries including a broken back. Gary always maintained his innocence. He was released from prison in 2012.

Scarecrow OD'd on the roof.

It was ripe for demolition and was razed to the ground to make way for social housing.

36 Albany Street

Spike lived here as did Katrin Parmentier, Tim Paine, Carl, Tracy and Napoleon. Katherine remembers fighting frequently with Napoleon over who took charge over what got played on the record player. Katherine wanted to play Johnny Thunders and Dean Martin while Napoleon wanted Motörhead and at an ear splitting volume.

48 Albany Street

Spike and Tim ran an anarchist bookshop in the basement although Tim recalls it being open for business on only a couple of occasions.

They also produced "The Rich Get Richer.... The Poor Get Poorer", issue (#8) of Class War. Issue number 10 "Victory To The Hit Squads" which was produced during the miner's strike 1984-1985 listed 36 Albany Street (Box CW) as a contact address.

Class War (the boisterous anarchist newspaper and political organisation) was co-founded by Ian Bone (once branded Britain's most dangerous man) and London Autonomist Martin Wright in 1983 after Ian moved from his home in Swansea (where he worked on a similar knockabout local paper called The Alarm) to London. Martin had thrown his lot in with Anarchy (he was a member of the Anarchy Collective) and Xtra!, posting regular contributions. Xtra! was published in North London from 1979 until 1982. There were 10 issues. A plan was sunk. Class War's no nonsense approach made it an instant hit with the nation's disaffected youth. At its height Britain's most unruly tabloid was selling 15,000 copies a week.

Spike and Tim also produced the mag "Heard It All Before".

Joseph Porter (and Sarah Lewington and Ania Skarzyńska) lived nearby at number 48. Edward Tudor-Pole lived opposite. Tim remembers drinking with him in a nearby hostelry.

Burn It Down Ballroom

3c Lithos Road

A warehouse space on Lithos Road. It was one of two Burn It Down Ballroom sites set up by the Kafe Kollaps collective (with the assistance of Berlin squatter punks Soldiers of Fortune) who also squatted another property on nearby Arkwright Road. The other was on the corner of Lymington Road and Finchley Road and is now a Jewish community hall.

Mark Edmonson (Youth In Asia) and Louise Harris aka Louise Challice (Youth In Asia and Hysteria Ward) stayed opposite in a top floor flat (leased from West Hampstead Short Life Housing Association) at 3c Lithos Road. Lou has fond memories of a street party. Her then band Hysteria Ward (and Decadent Few) played in the garden.

Amongst those bands who played at BIDB include The Mob (16/09/83), Chumbawamba + Poison Girls and Toxic Shock (05/10/83 at a benefit for Class War) and Hagar The Womb, Flowers in the Dustbin and Adrian and his Anal Birth Complex (10/12/83).

104A Tufnell Park Road

Tim Paine, Spike, Katrin Parmentier, Carl, Tracey and Rat from Peterborough lived here in 1984. Katherine and Spike lived in adjacent rooms on the ground floor. Tim, Carl, Rat and Tracey stayed on the floors above.

Spike was arrested at the second Stop The City. Ian Rawes née Slaughter (Pigs for Slaughter) came forward as a witness. As a result all charges against Spike were dropped.

Stop The City (STC) 1983-1984 was a series of grassroots anti-capitalist demonstrations targeting London's financial district. A 'Carnival Against War, Oppression and Destruction' if you will. Here's Al Puppy: "What I can add is that the idea for Stop the City came from Dave Morris – of McLibel trial fame, longest trial in English legal history – and London Greenpeace. It was organised from a house on Ickburgh Road, Upper Clapton, Hackney. Dave and others (including my future wife Pinki) had been given the house by the GLC so they could organise an anti-nuclear march from Faslane in Scotland to Greenham in Wiltshire."

The first mass mobilisation took place on the 29th of September 1983. 1500 protesters, many of them punks, descended on the "Square Mile". Penny Rimbaud takes up the story: "Royal exchange messengers had been prevented from operating. British Telecom workers had refused to work in the City. Restaurants and cafés had been stink-bombed; fur shops had been attacked; people had spent the whole day jamming telephone lines to banks and offices; there had been lie-ins and sit-downs, street theatre and music...acts of individual subversion from lock glueing to flying anarchist banners from the various statues that decorate the City." 200 people were arrested.

The following year on the 29th of March a bigger more robust demonstration took place resulting in 400 arrests.

Members of Crass Mick Duffield, Joy De Vivre and Andy Palmer collaborated on a one-hour film documentary about the second STC.

Two more demonstrations would take place - on the 31st of May 1984 and on the 27th of September albeit with mixed success.

Brixton Academy 18/04/87

"The Gathering of the 5,000" at Academy Brixton, Saturday the 18th of April 1987 proved to be a bit of a hot potato. What originally began as discussions around what is punk and what it meant in 1987 led to plans to put on a gig. Not just any gig but something far more spectacular.

Conflict grasped the nettle entering in to talks with Simon Parkes then owner of the South West London music venue Brixton Academy. Once negotiations with Parkes were complete which saw Colin posing as a Rough Trade employee (briefcase and slicked back hair), a deal was struck using stolen Rough Trade notepaper. The band (now joined by Steve Ignorant) pushed ahead anew. The gig was billed as a final tribute to Crass.

Spiralling costs meant they had to knuckle down to raise the money required. Rehearsals started in earnest.

The police finally caught wind of their plans mounting a huge operation involving 500 officers. Despite assurances to the contrary uniformed police were allowed in to the building. The police wanted to put a lid on it. To add insult to injury stall holders (of which there were many - London Greenpeace, Animal Liberation Front, Anti Apartheid Movement, Class War, Housmans Bookshop, Anti Fascist Action, Imprisoned Miners Support, Hunt Saboteurs Association, Compassion in World Farming, Leeds A.L.F./Bust Fund and Rape Crisis Centre with profits from the gig being split 50/50 between the Academy and the stall holders) were informed that they would have to pay a rental charge.

Ten tv screens would show films throughout Conflict's set.

One day to go and London hip hop act Three Wize Men opted to pull out. Benjamin Zephaniah stepped in to the breach.

April 18th! Coaches start arriving from all over the country. The Academy upped their security. 85 men and ten women. The mood was ominous. Thatcher on Acid took to the stage. Then it was Benjamin Zephaniah's turn. Conflict! During their performance trouble spilled on to the stage with some attendees set on violence. Academy security (some with dogs) beat up troublemakers and band members alike. The gig ended amid the chaos.

What happened next is unclear. Police started making arrests outside the hall. A full scale battle then ensued which saw attendees pitted against the police. Others went on the rampage smashing local shops. Fifty two people were arrested with others facing further penalties under the new Public Order Act.

The Academy had not been straight with the band and reneged on many of its promises. Perhaps most shocking of all was that they'd been serving beef burgers and not vegetarian food as agreed.

As a consequence the band was asked to pay £1000 for any damages caused. Afterwards Conflict was in effect facing a countrywide ban. Any gigs after that had to be performed in secret.

Commenting afterwards messers Ignorant and Jerwood said the gig created a window of opportunity. A beacon of hope if you like. Nothing like it had been tried before or since.

It was Kevin's Webb's very last performance with the band. Kevin died in France in 1999.

Conflict's set on the night was recorded and released as a double LP "Turning Rebellion In To Money" (MORT 30).

The tracks were as follows:

· A1 Banned From The UK

· A2 A Piss In The Ocean

· A3 Big A Little A

· A4 Increase The Pressure

· A5 The Serenade Is Dead

· A6 You Said That

· A7 From Protest To Resistance

- A8 To Whom It May Concern
- B1 Big Hands
- B2 So What
- B3 I Ain't Thick (It's Just A Trick)
- B4 G's Song
- B5 Contaminational Power
- B6 Cruise
- B7 Major General Despair
- B8 One Nation Under The Bomb
- C1 Bomb
- C2 Punk Is Dead
- C3 Rival Tribal Revel Rebel
- C4 Statement
- C5 The Day Before
- C6 This Is The A.L.F.
- C7 Tough Shit Mickey
- C8 Reality Whitewash
- C9 Working Class Rip-Off
- D1 Mighty And Superior
- D2 Do They Owe Us A Living
- D3 How Does It Feel
- D4 This Is Not Enough
- D5 Positive Junk
- D6 The System Maintains
- D7 Berkshire Cunt

In 1983 in a surprising turn of events Wattie from The Exploited in an attempt to smooth relations between the two bands invited Crass to join The Exploited (and South London skinhead band Serious Damage) on stage at The 100 Club 06/10/83. Annie Anxiety (Wattie and Annie were then in a romantic tryst) helped broker the deal.

Crass had played at the 100 Club once before – 19/06/81 with Flux of Pink Indians, Poison Girls and Annie Anxiety. Said gig was reviewed in the pages of music weekly Sounds June 20th 1981 by Edwin Pouncy.

Relations between Crass and The Exploited had always been chilly. For example Wattie had famously (on first LP "Punk's Not Dead" and possibly a retort to Crass song "Punk is Dead") declared that "Crass is just a bunch of fucking wankers!". On Crass' Christmas single "Merry Crassmas" Crass took a poke at The Exploited. "VERY MERRY CRASSMAS. HERE'S AN AMAZING XMAS MEDLEY OF CRASS'S GREATEST HITS. SUPER FUN FOR ALL THE FAMILY. PLUS...SUPER FUN TIME COMPETITION THAT EVERYONE CAN JOIN IN. HERE'S WHAT YOU DO...IT'S EASY. JUST LIST, IN ORDER, THE TITLES OF THE EXCITING CRASS SONGS ON THIS RECORD. THE FIRST THREE CORRECT

POSTCARDS TO BE RECEIVED WILL BE SENT THE FOLLOWING GREAT PRIZES...1ST PRIZE... BATHSALTS, 2ND PRIZE...ONE EXPLOITED SINGLE, 3RD PRIZE...TWO EXPLOITED SINGLES. HAVE FUN. SEND ENTRIES TO "CRASSMAS COMPETITION." PO BOX 279. LONDON N22."

As to the evening in question Crass performed a short 20 minute set much to the chagrin of the audience. The sieg-heiling throng were no less kind to Annie. Dave Lewer: "I was only about 13 at that time and felt pretty awful at the treatment Annie Anxiety received by the mixed audience of mostly punks and a lesser volume of skins who were hell bent on shouting abuse and throwing the contents of their plastic pint glasses at her. I can remember that after their set finished and as she left the stage I approached her and asked if she was OK – not much consolation I know after her being soaked with beer / spit and being viciously verbally abused."

In the end it was a brave attempt to bring two disparate groups closer together.

Brougham Road

Brougham Road is perhaps best known due to many of its celebrity tenants. It was home to a colourful troupe of hippies and punks. The east side of Brougham Road had been squatted since the early 1970s when it was abandoned by the GLC. Some of these properties had been licensed through Patchwork Housing Association (set up with the ethos to provide affordable social housing for single people) but were eventually handed over to the squatters.

Here's anarchist postman (and McLibel defendant) Dave Morris: "Well I was squatting in 64 Brougham Rd from 1974-1980. I was a postman in Islington. The house was very run down, with an old outside toilet and a sink for a kitchen. But we decorated the inside with posters, murals, press cuttings and inspiring slogans etc. I shared the place with Alan, a really decent and quiet young bloke who became an alcoholic in the late 1970s. Alan once got nicked when drunk at a train station wearing my post office jacket and wheeling about a post office trolley with bags of letters on it. This led to a raid on the house and some laughable police hysteria about him and me being in an anarchist train robbers gang... I testified in court that I had known nothing about it (and that probably nor did Alan), but he still got 6 months suspended (Mentioned in Albert Meltzer's autobiography, I Couldn't Paint Golden Angels). After I left I think he went downhill, and last I heard he tragically got run over by a bus.

The other bloke we shared with was Des Kelly from Ireland who I recall was writing a book... I have a mad photo of him trying to ride his bike UP our staircase. I did bump into him in Hackney 15 years later but can't remember what he was doing then. Spanish Elizabeth was next door I think. Zoundz folks moved into my place or next door after I left. I vaguely recall a guy (Bruce?) living at No 66 who did animation and who

72 Brougham Road   94 Brougham Road

told me he was working on an amazing path-breaking new film called 'Star Wars'.. it didn't sound to me like it would get anywhere with a crap name like that..."

Val Drayton also lived at 66 as did Joseph Porter in 1984 in a converted outhouse. But to begin with Joseph set up home at number 62 while his band compadre Steve Lake moved in to 64. Phil Ritchie, Min Kent and Cristina Mazzoni + Fish the cat were amongst some of sixty four's other tenants. Joseph's bedroom became a makeshift sound room and a go-to place to record.

The Mob who by this time had moved in to number 74 after picking themselves up and moving from Wiltshire recorded their "Ching" demo there.

Puppy Louise Challice, after being introduced to Tim Hutton (The Mob) and Joseph via Mark Wilson decides to record some music with Tim and Joseph. Penguin takes up the story: "One of the tracks on this personal tape is entitled 'Shalom' which means peace in Hebrew. This is a track that was written by Lou after she was badly attacked by two skinhead girls in Kilburn. Brett and Mick Lugworm from Puppy Mansions managed to get Lou to the Royal Free hospital in Hampstead to get

96 Brougham Road   *Penguin outside 96*

cleaned up and mended. The bedroom session has Josef on drums, Tim on guitar and Lou on second guitar and vocals.This line up ventured out of Josef's bedroom only twice Lou remembers. Once at a pub now forgotten when an amp blew up so no performance was completed, and once on the Fuck Off stage which was set up at Stonehenge Festival."

It was at number 62 that Zounds refined the songs for "Curse of Zounds". Joseph: "Several of the album tracks were worked out amongst those musty mattresses, likewise tardily, but speeded on their way by the tasty wares of yet another Bhagwanee recently discovered dealing near the Holloway Road:

"Shall we try 'Which Land?' again then?"

"Just hurry up with that spliff......""

Number 62 was demolished to build a road.

Andy Stratton aka Andy Barker (Null & Void) lived at number 72.

J.C. was the treasurer of Brougham Road housing co-op. He'd fled South Africa after evading military service and set up home at number 96. He'd also played drums with Riot Squad SA from Cape Town who recorded and released two singles via Final Hour Entertainment in 1981 and 1983. He built a homemade PA which became a familiar asset at LMC, Rosebery Peace Centre and Centro Iberico. In 1981 he was joined by Rob (Vex), Paul Van-Transit (The Snails, This Bitter Lesson and Faction) and Rob Challice (Faction). There Rob set up cassette label 96 Tapes and WOT! Distribution. He also eventually took over the reins at All The Madmen after Alistair Livingstone was summarily dismissed.

Another new and improved sound room was built in the basement of 96. Blyth Power took advantage of this recording "A Little Touch Of Harry In The Night" in December 1984. This cassette only release was released courtesy of 96 Tapes (96/15).

Neil Keenan (Blyth Power) lived next door at number 94 with his mother and sister Liz.

Apostles Andy Martin and Dave Fanning lived at 108. The 'Aktion Klub' was a makeshift music space set up by Dave and Andy at 108. Not a gig space per se. Members of HHC (Hackney Hell Crew) could often be found ensconced at 108. Pus (Goatsbreath), Ollie, Bucket, Alien, Martin, Simo and Mark Barabbas were amongst some of the regular visitors. A bit of a handful in the best possible way Penguin remembers one such tale of hijinks: "Watching, and participating, in the cutting of hair after several of the Hackney Hell Crew tumbled into 108 Brougham Road after two nights up on speed washed down with mixed cider and vodka drinks (them not me). They all wanted to get new hair cuts, while completely wired out, so the sticky hair clippers and rusty scissors were found around the place to cut hair (I was a participant cutting hair not getting hair cut). They wanted the worst haircuts ever known to man. That was the request. They, and I, tried our best, and in part we were successful in this quest. My hair was left untouched, I already had stupid enough hair!"

Another regular face at 108 was Robert Dellar. Robert produced 'Straight Up' fanzine as well as publishing several books via his small publishing empire Spare Change Books including Nick Blinkos 'Primal Screamer', 'Gobbing, Pogoing And Gratuitous Bad Language' and 'Seaton Point'. He was also involved with Wapping Autonomy Centre and Centro Iberico.

And then there was the jam sponge pudding on the kitchen ceiling.

108 Brougham Road

The bus garage behind Brougham Road was occupied by travellers in 1981-82. The Tibetan Ukrainian Mountain Troupe as they became known were "the creative, surreal. prankster Circus of the Stonehenge traveller scene". Convoy Steve. When the bus garage was demolished, several dwellings - 50-66 were knocked down.

Finally The Baader-Meinhof gang's (Red Army Faction) Astrid Proll became something of a local celebrity after she fled to London in August 1974. She stayed at various addresses including it is said Brougham Road at number 64. After four years on the run she was arrested on September 15th 1978. The Friends of Astrid Proll ran a high profile campaign to free her which included putting on a benefit at Acklam Hall on the 14th of November 1978 with The Passions and The Nips. Tom Vague: "I also remember Crass phoning up and desperately wanting to play at the gig (being anarchists I suppose they would), but there wasn't space on the bill for them. They were very disappointed. It was a good gig, well attended if I remember correctly."

It's 1979 and estranged ex-Hawkwind saxophonist Nik Turner sets about putting a new band together called Inner City Unit. The band's first single is an ode to Astrid Proll called "Solitary Astrid" later changed to "Solitary Ashtray" to fend off any controversy.

In June Astrid returns to West Germany where she is tried but not before serving a stretch in Brixton prison. She is one of three female inmates in an all male prison alongside Iris Mills (one of six defendants in the "Persons Unknown" trial). Astrid is sentenced to five and a half years.

In 1987 Hackney Council began evicting people. Some like Min and Mark Mob joined the Peace Convoy. Min was at "The Battle of the Beanfield" in 1985. Others found other similar accommodation.

Hollybush Hill E11

Hollybush Hill E11 was the postal address for industrial/experimental/electronics emporium Cause For Concern. This small London-based cassette label was run by Larry Peterson, "an effervescent character who writes like a crazed lunatic." Larry dipped in to the underground amassing a collection of strange and divergent artistic outpourings. He began releasing cassettes in 1982 with "Paranoia is Awareness" (CFC 001) a compilation that boasts an impressive collection of tracks from the likes of The Apostles, Assassins of Hope, Cause For Concern, Third Door From The Left, APF Brigade and Nocturnal Emissions. It proved to be the first of many releases. These included Third Door From The Left "Live 001 / Live 002" (CFC 003), The Apostles "The 2nd Dark Age" (CFC005), The Mob/Apostles "Live at the LMC" 22/01/83" (CFC 015), Throbbing Gristle "Nothing Short of a Total War" (CFC 016), Third Door From The Left "Face the Firing Squad" (CFC 017), we-be-echo "Ceza·Evi" (CFC 024), Nocturnal Emissions "Live at Ritzy Brixton 9 June 1983" (CFC026) "Stuff The Neighbours Play It Loud!" and Nocturnal Emissions "Chaos" (CFC LP 2).

Kevin Thorne (a musician in his own right with we be echo and Third Door From The Left) put his artistic skills to work by designing sleeves for several of CFC's releases.

To add to his resume Larry also ran (in conjunction with Apostles Andy Martin and Dave Fanning) The Recession Club 22-24 Ponsford Street E9 April 1983-January 1984. Larry's remit was choosing artists willing to perform.

In 1984 Larry + Andy and Dave recorded under the nom de plume The Omelettes.

Mike and Leon from Assassins of Hope stayed nearby. Issue number 6 of Scum fanzine was a collaboration between Mike and Leon and Larry and Ann Dee Martian.

In 1982 Mike played drums (tracks A1 to A2, A4 and B1) on The Apostles "Swimmers in the Sea of Life... The Fifth Demo". It was released the following year. Likewise AOH released their second demo (which also features Andy on vocals and lead guitar) the same year.

Let's hear from Leon, Larry and Kevin as they share their own personal recollections.

Larry: "Being into music very much, my first job at 15 I worked in a fringe theatre off Tottenham Court Road called Action Space in Chenies Street. It put on gigs, and I worked there for 2 years and joined a Performance Art/Music group called The Event Group, whom I later released their music on two cassettes from them plus members gave me solo stuff for my compilation cassettes. One big highlight was supporting New Order when they started and blowing them off stage in their hometown at The Ritzy Ballroom.

I was also very much into anarcho punk and any type of new music that was evolving around that time of the late 70s early 80s. I toyed with the idea of doing a fanzine called "Immobilise The Camera Detector" (words from The Hood, arch enemy from the first Thunderbirds episode). I absolutely loved fanzines and I used to buy loads of them plus buy the bands who were featured in them, cassettes and vinyl releases.

I was very, very open-minded to music. I dreamt about doing interviews with bands that I liked as I was really influenced by music on cassettes that you could buy from bands/artists by seeing their address and description of their music in Sounds music newspaper. There was a column called Cassette Pets. Bands used to sell their cassettes in this column very cheaply or you could send a cassette and a stamped address envelope and receive back their latest demo.

Strangely enough, if memory serves me, there was a band called APF Brigade. They would literally do a set in their garage that would be recorded live onto your cassette, so anybody who got a cassette from them had one individual performance. They said: "Thanks Larry" after the last song was played. Can you imagine this sort of thing today?"

The conversation then turns to how Larry met Assassins Leon and Mike. Larry: "I discovered I believe Assassins of Hope and The Apostles this way. Coincidentally, I always used to see a few punks and really cool looking females + their boyfriends (both brothers) plus dogs walking past my home once or twice a week and I used to think to myself who are these characters? Well, how about this twist of fate, this lot was The Assassins of Hope. And they advertised their cassette and I knew their address. They lived 9 doors away from me. Whaaaatttt!! I think I got up the courage to call on their door and I think their mum said no they don't live here, they only visit a few times a week, but eventually, I did get to know them and became best friends with some of them. How cool would that be, a band you liked living in your street. In fact, one of the members, Leon, moved back home. We became best buddies and we used to make music together and share our tales of what we were both doing. We spent most evenings playing our fave records, me bringing round Lustmord & Leon playing me the Clash, all the while experimenting with herbal varieties (that most hippies loved) plus Beatles, Gong and other stuff."

Leon: "By late 82 I stopped squatting and moved back home to my parents who had moved from Leytonstone to 44 Hollybush Hill in nearby Snaresbrook.

One evening I was getting off the tube in Snaresbrook and Larry came up to me on the platform and introduced himself. He told me he lived a few doors away from me in Hollybush Hill and that he had put Assassins of Hope on his compilation cassette. We chatted as we left the station and I was taken aback by Larry's effervescent enthusiasm for music and life in general .Just as we approached his house he said something to the effect that he liked all sorts of people but he couldn't stand Jews. I replied that I had no problem with anyone including Jewish people and Larry said that was good as he was Jewish himself. Larry was just testing me out. He then asked me in to his house for a cup of tea. That was the start of a friendship that has lasted over 40 years."

Larry: "They were wholly immersed in the anarcho punk scene and they liked nothing more than having a drink and the occasional scrap. Plenty of times I saw it kick-off in a pub somewhere. Especially their drummer. Mike, he just loved fighting. If someone insulted his girlfriend or was only a teeny bit rude to her, he would defend her honour and get right in with his girlfriend joining in too. If it wasn't Mike it was Peat who could be described as somewhat outspoken.

Wow, I had friends that acted like they lived in the old Wild West."

Leon: "By 1983 Ivan, Peat and Chantal were no longer in the band though we were all still friends. Around the time AOH were organising our new line up. Carl, a reggae loving punk soul boy joined us on guitar and we shortened the band name to The Assassins. Josie then decided to leave the band so we had no singer at this point until later that year when Gino joined us. So during the hiatus Andy Martin, who we were very friendly with by now, asked if he could sing and play guitar on some later AOH material that we had played live but never recorded .We liked the idea and so Mike and Leon joined Andy in Recession Studios to record the tracks. There was no talk of releasing it, it just seemed to be a bit of fun and it was nice to have those songs recorded for posterity.

In 1983 Assassins of Hope became more simply The Assassins and changed line up with eventually only Mike and Leon left of the original AOH. Carl was now on guitar and Gino on vocals. The Assassins did a number of rehearsals in Larry's front room while his parents were away on holiday and Larry became The Assassins manager. He got us lots of gigs including supporting The Meteors at Bowes Lyon House and got us a record deal with Backs Records of Norwich. We recorded a 12 inch 4 track ep called Hell Is For Heroes, which got to test pressing and was cut by George Peckham of Porky Prime Cut fame. Larry: The band also designed a fantastic artwork cover with many colours and this was going to be quite expensive but sadly and I can't remember why but it never got past the test pressing stage." Leon: "Unfortunately Backs got cold feet and reneged on the record release so there are just a few test pressings in existence.

After a couple of years Gino and Carl left the band and the last Assassins incarnation with Lol on vocals and guitar and Dan on 2nd guitar gigged extensively and recorded 2 cassettes - Lust For Life (no connection to Mr Pops oeuvre) in 1986 and Never Been A Killer, in 1987. After that three of The Assassins formed a more Motorhead, Pink Fairies, early Metallica influenced punk band called Swine but that's another story ".

Larry: "And so it evolved, I ditched the fanzine idea, but went with the idea of releasing a compilation cassette of my favourite bands that I had recently been exposed to and I advertised them through the fanzines I knew, plus sell some through the odd gig I went to. This cassette was called Paranoia is Awareness and it did extremely well. I was shocked at how it took off. I was potty about going to gigs. I maybe went to 3 or 4 a week. I once kept a list and I knew I'd hit 500 in a few years. And if the band were not helpful enough, I would ask to release their cassettes or put them on compilation cassettes. It grew so big I bought myself a double speed, double cassette recorder that could record a C60 in 15 minutes. I used to stay up very late at night recording the label's cassettes. I had fantastic artwork designed by Kevin Thorne and I spent good money getting his covers printed at Little A printers lithographically. Kevin's artwork in my opinion could be considered to be the best and most striking artwork around and for a young 17-18 year old kid to use for his cassette label, I am certain it opened many doors for me as most underground vinyl & cassette artwork was very DIY."

Kevin: "In the early 1980's I was communicating with Larry Peterson of Cause For Concern. I think initially to provide a track for his "A Sudden Surge Of Power" cassette, and somehow I ended up designing the cover. This was way before desktop publishing, so everything was cut 'n' paste. Luckily I worked at a company doing the artwork for magazines, so I had access to typesetting machines. I collected interesting images, and found a suitable one to use for the cover. Later, Larry asked me to design covers for Throbbing Gristle's "Nothing Short Of A Total War" cassette, The Mob/The Apostles "Live At The LMC", Nocturnal Emissions "Live At Ritzy" and his "Stuff The Neighbours Play It Loud" ep. The images all came from my box of saved images.

Larry provided vocals on "Looking For The Light", a we be echo song on the 1986 cassette "Nothing Left", released on Mystery Hearsay."

Larry: "I put out over 30 releases out on cassette, plus I then released a 7 inch vinyl single and a live LP by Nocturnal Emissions, and I became the manager of the Assassins of Hope.

I then met a girl and I wanted to spend more time just being normal, being a boyfriend so I kind of wanted it to wane at that point of time, but I actually got more involved in my local scene and joined a band as singer called "Many Happy Returns". We had a track on a miners benefit album at the time called Here We Go (on Sterile Records in 1985). Search up Many Happy Returns on YouTube, with their track SING. The Assassins are on this too!

A year or two later...

I squatted with Ann Dee Martin & Ian Rawes aka Ian Slaughter. Me and Andy gave Ian a lot of stress as he worked very early mornings and went to bed about 9pm. In hindsight the idea of us living in a house with a guy who went to bed that early wasn't a great idea, "lots of keep the noise down" at 9.30pm.

How I met The Apostles was at a gig for the first time. I asked them if they had any cassettes for sale. They said yes, we have a few so I said do you want me to go and sell the others for you at this gig. Could have been a gig of The Fall, or one of their own gigs, anyway I sold a few at other gigs too. And like most bands, they're not very upfront about selling their own product so I went around the crowd and sold quite a few. Naturally they were delighted. My favourite cassette of theirs was called "The Second Dark Age" so I released it myself and it gained them new exposure, plus introducing Andy further into my world of difficult music, but he was the master already, György Ligeti and Stockhausen he told me he liked.

I was with them when they recorded their first EP. It was recorded in Recession Studios in Hackney and they saved their own money up for it. (Ann Dee) Andy worked very hard in an Anarchist Printers in Wapping called Little A. He religiously scrimped and saved for this. Quite admirable. He never allowed himself any luxuries.

Again, when there were gigs, I sold quite a few singles for them plus through my own channels, because obviously I had a cassette label. I brokered a deal with Rough Trade for them and sold 600 of the 1000 singles. It's true I sold the lion's share of their first release. It's something I have never been given any credit for, but this is the first time the subject is raised in over 40 years and the reason is further below.

This from that day onwards meant that The Apostles would go on the journey of releasing countless 7 inch single E.Ps. I think they had the distribution now set up with Rough Trade for the remaining ones, but I had only partial distribution to do with the EP2, 3, 4 and 5. So let's just say, I opened the door for them.

I would also like to say publicly and I'm not mentioning names, that I was going to go away to work abroad for six months. Before I left, someone approached me and asked me and said, I can get a deal and release the Mob/Apostles live cassette on vinyl plus Nothing Short Of A Total War by Throbbing Gristle, which was already on my label and I had been given permission to release. I said to this fella look I'm going away in a week. I've got nothing against it. I've known you quite a while and I trust you so I will leave it with you. It's okay with me, all I would like out of it is 6 copies of each LP, no money at all, but you must get permission. The guy said yeah, yeah, yeah, yeah!!

I went away abroad and months later I received a letter at home which my mum forwarded to me which was a terribly strong letter from Andy Martin, telling me that I had bootlegged the tape onto vinyl & how despicable I was. As my memory is not good, I cannot remember if I replied but if I did, I would've explained the story in full. My mistake was to trust somebody. It was just a youthful mistake. It was very upsetting. I had helped their band like no other had before and most importantly lost their friendship. I still think about it all the time. It was my first serious fall out with someone and not entirely my fault. On a different note, the Throbbing Gristle album got destroyed so any copies around are extremely rare as they didn't want this album bootlegged either."

Of The Recession Club he says: "As I remember it, the guy who owned the studio had rehearsal rooms, one was big with lots of lights in, ideal for bands to professionally showcase their act. He said I rarely rent this room out, but if you want it for the night, bring bands down & have a gig venue, I just want the night's room hire money, which was reasonable.

So I mainly oversaw which bands performed there. Admission was extremely cheap, sometimes taking what entrants could afford. Bring your own booze. It was well attended every week and I remember most bands being excited in doing their first ever gigs and everybody was appreciative and a friendly vibe was present each week."

Brixton Ace 08/10/83

On the 8th of October 1983 Conflict, Vex, Anthrax, Lost Cherrees, Hagar the Womb, Moet The Poet, Omega Tribe and The Partisans (who'd relocated to The Big Smoke from Bridgend) performed in front of an adoring Brixton crowd. The gig saw The Partisans cross the floor if you will. Firmly ensconced in the Oi! camp it was somewhat of a departure for the Welsh punkers. It saw them start to shake that tag. Hot on the heels of their "Blind Ambition" single, six songs from their feisty performance made it on to side 2 of their new LP "Time Was Right" (PART LP 1) on Cloak & Dagger in 1984.

- B1 17 Years

- B2 Change

- B3 Arms Race

- B4 Come Clean

- B5 Overdose

- B6 Partisans

Like The Partisans, Conflict's performance was also recorded for posterity and shaped side B of their second LP "Increase The Pressure" (LP MORT 6) on Mortarhate in 1984.

The track listing is as follows:

- B1 The Positive Junk

- B2 The System Maintains

- B3 The Berkshire Cunt

- B4 The Guilt and the Glory

- B5 Stop The City

- B6 One Nation Under A Bomb

· B7 Blind Attack

· B8 Vietnam Serenade

· B9 Blood Morons

· B10 Exploitation

· B11 Whichever Way You Want It

The gig received a tepid review in the pages of Sounds. In it journo Johnny Waller begins by highlighting a shrieking error: "The last time Hagar the Womb were reviewed in this rag, they were laughingly accused of being fascists (which they're so obviously NOT). This time I accuse them of being brilliant (which they so nearly are!)." He called them: "A modern recreation of X Ray Spex." About The Partisans he writes: "The Partisans came and went with their brand of fast, loud but not unattractive punk-thrash... ". Turning his attention to Lost Cherrees he writes: "However, they injected some earnest enthusiasm into their performance and stand unique as the only punk band I've ever witnessed covering a Monkees song (and the unlikely 'Pleasant Valley Sunday' at that!)". About Moet the Poet he writes: "Like a cross between Mark Miwuirdz and Mark Perry he was sharp, direct and deliberately repetitive with abstract lyrics that could have come straight out of a Fall song." Finally he says this about Conflict: "Conflict undoubtedly have the potential, the ability and the vision to do something startling and innovative."

Paul Castle (Punk Lives! #11) puts a far more positive spin on the evening's events. "One of the most enjoyable gigs for ages, and a real treat with so many good bands on the show all for £1.50. This again showed Conflict's determination to do things their way, and not be prepared to dance to anyone else's tune. The tune is now Conflict's. Let's hope they keep it that way!"

The Ace also played host to Southern Death Cult (10/07/82) and (07/03/83), Poison Girls (05/03/83), Sex Gang Children and Brigandage (17/03/83), Brigandage (31/03/83), Conflict, Annie Anxiety, Destructors, Hagar the Womb, Drill, Votrex and Systematix (Artists For Animals Presents - An anarchist ball for the Animal Liberation Front and Anti-Whaling Fund 26/05/83), Blood and Roses (31/08/83) and Conflict, Vex,

Icons of Filth and Hagar The Womb (17/03/84 which was the culmination of a 20 date nationwide tour ahead of the release of Increase The Pressure which hit the shops in April).

Tony Puppy aka Tony Drayton wrote a fair appraisal of the animal lib gig at the Ace for punk glossy "Punk Lives!" #7.

Punk Lives was a popular music magazine 1982/3. It was part of the Kerrang! publishing group under the editorial leadership of Alf Martin. While it catered for a more mainstream punk audience it also included regular contributions from Tony Puppy (Tony interviewed cover stars The Mob in #5 and Eltham's finest Conflict in #6, Alien Sex Fiend #6, Sex Gang Children #10 and Flesh For Lulu #11), Al A aka Alistair Livingstone (reporting on the final gig at Westbourne Road's Centro Iberico in #4 and Black Sheep Housing Co-op #6 as well as interviewing Blood and Roses in #5), and Richard Kick aka Richard Cabut who talks to Twisted Nerve #11. Penny Rimbaud also wrote a report from the frontlines at Stop The City in #10. Rubella Ballet were interviewed (by Kilty McGuire) in #3.

Two songs from the Southern Death Cult performance ('Faith' and 'The Crypt') 10/07/82 were recorded and broadcast on Channel 4 programme Whatever You Want 22/11/82. Whatever You Want was a popular youth and current affairs programme presented by Keith Allen 08/11/1982 - 28/03/1983.

13 James Street

Once the humble abode of Tony Drayton, Jeremy Gluck, Dave Sex Gang, Bob Short and Brett Puppy. Tony: "The last issue of Ripped & Torn I was involved with was issue 17, which is dated March 1979. At that time I moved out of Frestonia and into a large squatted complex in Covent Garden, an interlinked series of shop fronts, warehouses and rooms that stretched around James Lane and Long Acre." Brett remembers teasing passers by by dangling an imitation pigeon from a window on a piece of string. Whenever they tried to reach for it he'd twist it from their grasp. Opposite, above Covent Garden tube station, were the offices of music weekly Sounds. Bob Short: "Across James Street, behind a façade of plywood and corrugated iron, was a huddle of old shops and offices awaiting demolition. The last eviction notices had been served and the wrecking ball was booked. All that remained was a motley crew of squatters awaiting the sheriff's men."

Tony's head was turned by a musical group Anarchist United Mystics who regularly held jam sessions in the basement. Part of a spiritual awakening if you like. Occultism became a prime mover in his life. Tony: "There was an old black gentleman living in the building who was very into Crowley and magick and the Illuminati. He gave me a copy of an ancient edition of The Cosmic Trigger by Robert Anton Wilson." Tony also recalls seeing Genesis (P-Orridge) discussing arcane matters in Atlantis Bookshop around this time.

On June 15th at "The Squat" following Tony's arrest on squatting charges, a benefit gig was swiftly arranged, the monies from which would be split between Tony's fines and Ripped & Torn. The Barracudas, Royal Family and Charge were the star turns.

Kardboard Box and Wood Green Arts Centre

In 1986 band Gutrot began squatting an abandoned DHSS (Department of Health and Social Security) building at 1 Kings Road, Wood Green N22. Gutrot were Steve Telford (formerly of Scottish punkers AOA), Dalb, Tim Knight and Darryn Garlinge. Drummer Darryn would later join up with pals Axegrinder.

They tore down adjoining walls. Offices became bedrooms. Members of the Hackney Hell Crew cleared an area for gigs and built a stage using estate agents' "For Sale" signs. Active Conspiracy who ran the gigs in tandem with Gutrot provided the PA. What became known as the Kardboard Box became a fulcrum for the North London scene.

11/12/86. Extreme Noise Terror, Atavistic, Ripcord, Axegrinder, Karma Sutra, Blower, Active Conspiracy, Gutròt, Rest In Pain and Zoggers played a massive blowout at the Kardboard Box.

Micky Russo cooked up two crates of cauliflower which he'd found round the back of Sainsbury's, charging 50p a plate. All monies went to the ALF. However an argument ensued after Steve (Telford) refused to put 50p in the donation box. Accusations flew and a fight broke out.

A group of Irish travellers took up residency in the car park stealing lecky from the Kardboard Box. Things took a nasty turn when they turned over a squat in Wood Green stealing Christmas gifts.

Conflict and Exit-Stance also played at the Box.

The track "Special Brew" from Axegrinder's "1987 "Grind The Enemy" demo is an affectionate tribute to the Kardboard Box.

According to Dalb, Steve would don marigold gloves to do the dishes in order to keep his hands dirty.

After the Kardboard Box was evicted Gutrot took over an old dance centre, the Zena Letchworth School of Dance, Station Road, Wood Green which became known as The Ballet School. Deviated Instinct played there on the 21st of March 1987.

Wood Green Arts Centre or Ye Olde Arts Centre as it's sometimes called (on Redvers Road N22) was an old carpet warehouse. It was squatted by Gutrot + Bill Auld and Animal from God Told Me To Do It. GTMTDI (Sean, Bill, Bug and Animal) or GOD to their most devoted fans, were self-publicists, master manipulators and chiefs of scandal. They once famously squatted the Libyan People's Bureau in London in 1986.

GTMTDI played a one-off gig (at Wood Green Arts Centre) as Bladder All Stars. Other appointed gigs included Chumbawamba, No Defences, Assessment and Moses and the Desert Wellies (06/09/85), State Hate (14/09/85), Blyth Power, National Interest and God Told Me To Do It (a benefit for Unwaged Fightback 26/10/85), AOA, State Hate, Eat Shit and Sons of Bad Breath (31/10/85), Stupids, AYS, Only Human and God Told Me To Do It (02/11/85), Antisect, DIRT, Sacrilege and Sedition (08/11/85), Liberty, Hex and Danbert Nobacon (14/11/85) and The Ex and Newtown Neurotics (15/11/85).

The police were permanently ensconced in the front garden.

Unfortunately neither of these properties have survived the rigours of time.

Zig Zag Squat 18/12/82

The Apostles. Photo Graham Burnett.

In December 1982 Crass squatted the empty Rainbow Theatre in Finsbury Park. The plan? To stage a 24 hour free concert. This followed a frosty reaction among club owners in regards Crass playing in the capital after their anti-Falklands single "How Does It Feel?" fuelled controversy in both the press and parliament.

Security and police had other ideas however and quickly and rudely removed the squatting party. Down but not out they recouped their losses and within no time at all had secured another building – the Zig Zag club on Westbourne Road.

"Squatting this venue is not a last ditch stand to get a gig, the music business would love us all to be down at the Venue paying their bar prices: On the contrary, we hope that today's gathering will provide inspiration and impetus to people everywhere to take similar opportunities and open up and take back the property that belongs to us all ... We hope that today we will be able to demonstrate that together we can begin to reclaim that which is ours . . . Freedom, free food, free shelter, free information, free music, free ideas . . . Freedom to do whatever doesn't infringe on the freedom of others."

The electricity was turned on and the building made safe, a kitchen serving hot vegetable soup was set up and the main hall readied with posters, flags and banners. FREE BEER!

"Today is a chance to drop old constricting roles and values. A chance to get a taste of music, dancing, love and real anarchy (not the text book type). A chance to tap the reservoir of energy and inspiration that we don't often bother to break through to. A chance to take control of our own lives from the ticket touting music biz; from the money grabbing capitalists, from the multi-national corporations, from the power mad politicians, the democrats, Eurocrats, bureaucrats, from all that crap and prove that we can do it and live it better ourselves".

Crass threw open the doors to all and sundry and turn up they did. Answering the call people turned up in their droves. A ragtag army of the disenfranchised and dispossessed. Bands rallied. A veritable who's who of the anarcho-punk glitterati pledged their support. Those that did (each band did a 30 minute turn) included Faction, D and V, Omega Tribe, Lack of Knowledge, Sleeping Dogs, Apostles, Youth In Asia, Null and Void, Amebix, Soldiers of Fortune, The Mob, Polemic Attack, Poison Girls, Conflict, Flux of Pink Indians, Annie Anxiety, Crass and DIRT. This would prove to be DIRT's final gig. At least in the interim. Flux's Martin Wilson stood in for Fox who made a hasty exit half way through their set.

The gig marked a significant historical moment. It offered a glimpse of one possible future, one without rules and restrictions. A kernel of hope. All we have to do is step through that door.

Winston Smith ended his review in Sounds (January 1st 1983) with these words: "NOBODY WAS hurt, no-one suffered, nobody ruled and no-one was governed. For 24 hours Crass had achieved their much-ridiculed vision of a peaceful, creative Anarchy in the most fantastically triumphant, clean, efficient way anyone could have ever imagined possible.

This was truly a Christmas on Earth.

It won't be forgotten."

However the day wasn't without its share of controversy. At one point five skinheads pushed their way to the front of the stage attacking a solitary 15 year old Asian boy who they gave a severe beating. No one tried to help which astonished and enraged Andy Martin. To their credit Penny and Andy from Crass did jump up to help. Colin Conflict gave the remaining skinheads a pasting. The skinheads ran off. The incident however deepened the rift between The Apostles and those whose politics took a more pacifist turn.

I asked one of the attendees Graham Burnett (New Crimes zine) about his recollections of the day. Graham: As I remember the Zig Zag Squat gig was almost a year to the day after Crass had played at the Wapping Autonomy Centre in December 1981, and so much had happened in the UK during those twelve months. The political climate had definitely hardened: the Tories had been in charge for three and a half years by then, the police were getting more and more powers, and were clamping down on any organised opposition or protest. I think The Falklands War in the summer of 82 had brought things to a head, a totally avoidable conflict with Argentina that cost thousands of lives but also unleashed a tidal wave of jingoism, patriotism and previously waning public support for Thatcher and her policies. It was a dark time if your ideals were radical or even a bit politically progressive, and there was definitely an air of despondency and despair pervading the anarcho-punk scene. It became inward looking and increasingly factionalised and Crass themselves weren't immune either. I mean, they were never exactly a comedy act, but there was always a sense of community and hope at their gigs, and dare I say an element of fun or even dry humour, but after the Falklands War there was "Iron in the Soul," with a kind of bitterness and desperation pervading records like 'How Does It Feel To Be The Mother Of A Thousand Dead' and 'Yes Sir I Will' that wasn't there earlier. I think Crass and some of the other bands associated with anarcho-punk like Flux of Pink Indians, Poison Girls, etc realised this, and decided to put on an event at the end of the year that would bring folks together and maybe lift the spirits, that despite everything there was still room for celebration and even inspiration. I'd also gone through some personal changes during that year, although I still liked the ideas of anarcho-punk I was also becoming interested in a lot more dance and rap music, the New York club scene stuff that was still quite underground but starting to be heard in the UK. So I turned up at the Zig Zag wearing a smart looking suit, white shirt and tie I'd bought for about a quid in a jumble sale, and found myself possibly the only person there that wasn't dressed in black army surplus gear in various stages of disintegration. I'd taken about five steps into the building when a couple of crusty punks came up and accused me of being a police spy - because, of course, if you were going to infiltrate a gathering of several hundred spikey-topped anarchist punk squatters, dressing like a smart soul boy is exactly what you'd do if you wanted to blend seamlessly into the crowd...

Omega Tribe. Photo Graham Burnett.

But apart from that it was an excellent all day event, featuring some of the best anarcho-punk bands of the era each playing a half hour set across the day, including Poison Girls, Conflict, The Mob, Omega Tribe, Youth In Asia, The Apostles, Lack of Knowledge, Null And Void, Polemic, Amebix, DIRT, D & V and of course Crass.

The original plan was to put the event on at The Rainbow in Finsbury Park which had stood empty for a few years. Members of Crass, The

Apostles and other squatting organisations had managed to get access to the building a few days beforehand and put the word out that an event would be coming up at the weekend. This was way before the internet or social media of course, so it was mainly by word of mouth. Unfortunately the squatters got evicted from that building at short notice so there was a very hasty change of plan - as I remember you had to call a phone number the night before to get the details of the new venue, it was all very last minute and secretive, yet hundreds of people still turned up... How ever did we manage before WhatsApp and Facebook, ha ha!

I recall a real party atmosphere, it wasn't just about the bands, but about what people can achieve and how we can demonstrate mutual aid when we self-organise. There was no admission charge, no age restrictions, no door staff or bouncers and everybody was welcome. A makeshift kitchen was set up, distributing free vegetable soup and cups of tea, plus a stall run by Housmans Bookshop selling and distributing anarchist books and literature, and an abandoned supply of beer found in the basement which was duly distributed to the masses. The sense of community was well and truly back, and revitalised the sense of possibility, paving the way for actions like Stop The City the following year. As a leaflet distributed on the day explained: "Squatting this venue is not a last ditch stand to get a gig, the music business would love us all to be down at the Venue paying their bar prices: On the contrary, we hope that today's gathering will provide inspiration and impetus to people everywhere to take similar opportunities and open up and take back the property that belongs to us all. We hope that today we will be able to demonstrate that together we can begin to reclaim that which is ours . . . Freedom, free food, free shelter, free information, free music, free ideas . . . Freedom to do whatever doesn't infringe on the freedom of others. It is up to us together to make it work. Treat others as you would expect to be treated and leave the place as it was when you arrived."

Which, despite the hundreds of people present with nobody policing us or telling us what to do, is precisely what happened. The Zig Zag squat was truly Anarchy in Action!"

The Robey

The Sir George Robey, 240 Seven Sisters Road was a popular public house and music venue. This mid-nineteenth century hostelry originally called The Clarence Tavern was renamed in popular music hall entertainer Sir George Robey's (1869-1954) honour in 1968. Its down at heel facade and interior wouldn't win any awards and its toilets were famous.

For our purposes several anarcho bands played on its tiny stage including Flux of Pink Indians, The System and Hagar The Womb (18/10/82), Blood and Roses (1982), Rubella Ballet. Chaos and Youth In Asia (07/09/82), Subhumans (07/02/83), Rubella Ballet (11/02/83), Conflict, Hagar The Womb and Vex (1983), Flowers in the Dustbin, Corpse and The Seers (10/08/83), and two days later Flowers In The Dustbin, Omega Tribe and Youth In Asia (12/08/83), Blyth Power, Thatcher On Acid and We Are Going To Eat You (18/12/86) Final gig with Curtis, Neil and Andy. Flowers In The Dustbin (23/01/87), Axegrinder (1987), Blyth Power and Hysteria Ward (03/03/87), The Astronauts (30/04/87), MDC and Culture Shock (05/12/87), Napalm Death, Bolt Thrower and Cerebral Fix (04/08/88), Bolt Thrower, Hellbastard, Doom, Energetic Krusher, Scum Children and Bomb Disneyland (1988) and Instigators (22/09/88).

In 1996 it changed hands and became part of the Mean Fiddler Group. It closed in 2004. It was eventually demolished in 2015.

The Subhumans set 07/02/83 was released on a single sided cassette (Bluurg23) on Bluurg Tapes.

"Banned From The Roxy"

The Roxy 41-43 Neal Street WC1 was one of punk's early salvos. Britain's very first punk club would reverberate to the sounds of a brand new music featuring many of the country's up and coming punk bands. The Clash, The Adverts, The Heartbreakers, Penetration, The Models, Siouxsie, UK Subs and Crass were just a few.

But let's back up a bit. The idea of opening a punk club in Covent Garden was first hatched by Andrew Czezowski, Susan Carrington and Barry Jones. The building had previously been a gay club called Chaguaramas and it was Gene October (male model and punk rock provocateur) who first brought the vacant two story building to their attention. No sooner had they got their foot in the door Andrew swiftly arranged three gigs in December 1976. On December 14th he put on his young proteges Generation X. Then a mere 24 hours later he put on The Heartbreakers hot off the Anarchy tour. Next he put on Susan Ballion aka Siouxsie and Generation X on the 21st. However the club didn't receive its official baptism until January 1st 1977 when The Clash and Chelsea took centre stage.

In 1977 I hope I go to heaven

'Cause I been too long on the dole

And I can't work at all

Danger stranger

You better paint your face

No Elvis, Beatles, or The Rolling Stones

In 1977

Gigs came thick and fast. Damned, Eater, The Jam, Wire, The Cortinas, Vibrators, Subway Sect, and more. "American Week" featured Stateside artists Cherry Vanilla, Wayne County and The Electric Chairs and Johnny Thunders and the Heartbreakers. A scene coalesced around the little club and for 100 days it bravely soldiered on. A denizen of youthful rebellion. Free and unabashed.

Don Letts was the resident DJ whose reggae record collection turned on the punks and opened their ears. He was also something of a budding filmmaker. His Super 8 movies were a snapshot of the period featuring many of its colourful characters and bands. In 1978 "The Punk Rock Movie" was cut and hit cinemas.

The hastily put together "Live at The Roxy WC2" (which included live tracks from Slaughter and the Dogs, The Unwanted, Wire, Adverts, Johnny Moped, Eater, X-Ray Spex and Buzzcocks) compilation was released to great acclaim reaching number 24 in the UK album charts.

April 1977. Whilst its glory days may have been behind it, the club stuttered on under new management. A new wave of bands took up the mantle. The Bears, Menace, The Valves, The Wasps, The Killjoys, Ed Banger and the Nosebleeds, The Zips and Sham 69. However for the purposes of this book let's look at Crass. Crass played at The Roxy on three occasions - 27/08/77, 22/09/77 and 30/09/77. It was after one such drunken melee that they were banned. Penny wrote a pointed response in the pages of Crass mouthpiece International Anthem #1 "Crass at The Roxy, he falls articulating on the skinned dog". In it he takes no prisoners. "Middle-class taste has, with it's infinite ability to adapt and to consume, accepted punk as a music and, encouraged by neat commercial packaging, has been able to totally ignore the real issues from which it originated. The political and social aspects of punk have been swamped by commercial considerations. Too eagerly, too quickly, too neatly have the young revolutionaries been sold the party line..........

Play as you earn.

The Green-back dream.

The Beatles are dead, the Stones are dead, Dylan is dead and so are the Rolls Royce punkers. A torn sweat shirt is a statement not a fashion. No one would have believed that fashion could buy the line, but it has. Punk has become radical Manhattan chic, encouraged by its super-stars who bought their ticket, but never got on the plane.

Yes, they talk of revolution, but it's from the back of a limousine and all the time some uncle Tom changes head for them and sees that the wheels are turning. They talk of revolution from the safety of the stage, protected by their position, their privilege, their armoured minds. Well, they climbed on my shoulders to get there and right now I'm moving away.

Wham. See?

And the limousine runs on cash and the cash flows and the record sales grow and I don't see Radio Ethiopia free anyone in Harlem, no way, the words of revolution resound across the pinewood furniture of America's dream, dissent and Bacardi, on the rocks, and no one cares a fuck. Not one of those middle-class consumers would dare show their face in the Roxy, even if now the Roxy is a tame commercial rip-off where tired ex-blues bands pump out timid and sterilised versions of what they think punk might have been. Posers. What kind of revolution is this? Everyone's living off the brief six months of Roxy revolution and imagining the battle's over. It is in one sense, the generals have retreated behind the lines, but there's still an army out there and they'd best not forget it. Everyone's waiting to see it happen, well it ain't going to if we're waiting on orders from above. Johnny Rotten had his arms and legs cut off by Tin Pan Alley, so he won't be back, nor will the rest of the elite, and they're all hanging about for a slice of meat."

He goes on: "Punk ain't music, it's a way of thought. Punk ain't a fashion, it's a way of being, it's anarchy in the U.K. the U.S.A. where-ever, and that isn't tuned guitars and clever vocal lines any more than it's limousines at the stage door of CBGBs. Oh, you Monroes how you line the corridors to the morgue.

If the first-wave punkers. concorde anarchists, velvet zippies, have sold out and become property in some wanked out economic system, it's up to the second wave to fight a hard battle, this time it's against an army wearing the same uniform."

"Outside on the wet London pavement we air our discontent. It is one o'clock and everyone's closing down for the night and this is 1977. We vow that next time we won't pay, it's our music, why should we, the audience and performer pay for it? We write graffiti on the Roxy wall to let them know that we are still alive, even if we are cold."

The experience also served as inspiration for song "Banned From The Roxy", track 8 on Crass' first record "Feeding of the 5000" (521984) in 1978.

International Anthem: A Nihilist Newspaper for the Living (1978-1993) was a radical newspaper. It ran for five issues. Gee produced issue 1 while she was still living in New York. It became the unofficial mouthpiece of Crass and featured contributions from Penny, Eve, Joy, Hari Nana aka Andy and Dave King. Dave is perhaps best known as the designer of the Crass symbol which he designed as the frontispiece for Christ's Reality Asylum.

Banned From The Roxy

Banned from the Roxy... O.K.

I never much liked playing there anyway

They said they only wanted well behaved boys

Do they think guitars and microphones are just fucking toys?

Fuck 'em, I chosen to make my stand

Against what I feel is wrong with this land

They just sit there on their overfed arses

Feeding off the sweat of less fortunate classes

They keep their fucking power cause their finger's on the button

They've got control and won't let it be forgotten

The truth of their reality is at the wrong end of a gun

The proof of that is Belfast and that's no fucking fun

Seeing the squaddy lying in the front yard

Seeing the machine guns resting on the fence,

Finding the entrance to your own front door is barred

And they've got the fucking nerve to call it defence

Seems their defence is just the threat of strength

Protection for the privileged at any length

The government protecting their profits from the poor

The rich and the fortunate chaining up the door

Afraid that the people may ask for a little more

Than the shit they get The shit they get

The shit they get The shit they get

The shit they get The shit they get

The shit they get The shit they get

Defence? Shit, it's nothing less than war

And no one but the government know what the fuck is for

Oh yes they say it's defence

they say it's decency

Mai Lai, Hiroshima, know what I mean?

The same fucking lies with depressing frequency

They say "We had to do it to keep our lives clean"

Well whose life?

Whose fucking life?

Who the fuck are they talking to?

Whose life?

Whose fucking life?

I tell you one thing, it ain't me and you

And their system, christ, they're everywhere

School, army, church, corporation deal

A fucked up reality based on fear

A fucking conspiracy to stop you feeling real

Well ain't got me

I'd say their fucking wrong

I ain't quite ready with my gun

but I've got my song...

Banned from the Roxy, well O.K.

I never much liked playing there anyway

Guns!

White Lion, Putney

The White Lion (1887-2019) 14-16 Putney High Street is a Grade ll listed public house.

On the 25th of April 1978 at The White Lion in what was only their sixth ever gig Crass played with The Crack and UK Subs. Crass: "Throughout the long, lonely winter of 77/78 we played regular gigs at The White Lion, Putney with the UK Subs. The audience consisted mostly of us when the Subs played and the Subs when we played. Sometimes it was disheartening, but usually it was fun. Charley Harper's indefatigable enthusiasm was always an inspiration when times got bleak, his absolute belief in punk as a peoples' music had more to do with revolution than McClaren and his cronies could ever have dreamt of."

It was around this period after The Roxy debacle that Crass began to take themselves far more seriously, eschewing the use of alcohol and cannabis before a performance and wearing black military fatigues on and off stage. Their onstage multi-media set up was deliberately provocative. Films, banners and leaflets outlining their ideas were part of an overall assault on the senses and imagination. There was none of the usual pomp of most rock gigs. No frills. No lighting rig.

The broken rifle symbol was adopted by Crass. It is an internationaly recognised peace symbol that dates from 1909 from De Wapens Neder (Down With Weapons), the paper of the International Antimilitarist Union.

Crass would return to the White Lion three years later accompanied by DIRT 17/12/81. In 1982 The Mob played there (24/04/82) followed by Rubella Ballet (29/04/82), Flux of Pink Indians and The System (20/05/82), DIRT and Youth In Asia (10/06/82), Conflict (17/06/82), Flux of Pink Indians, The System and Subhumans (01/07/82), Lost Cherrees (15/07/82) and Rudimentary Peni (05/08/82).

The Subhumans set 01/07/82 was committed to tape and released by Subhumans "London Putney White Lion" (BLUURG 19) in 1982.

DIRT's second vinyl offering was a live 12" disc recorded at New Half Moon, Stepney on the 5th of April 1982. Lack of Knowledge and Anthrax were also added to the roster that night. DIRT took two stabs at recording. I spoke to Deno who takes up the story: "Firstly the reason we recorded the live 12"twice was because everyone in the crowd could see we were recording the set and for some reason decided to be quiet with little reaction apart from some applause like they were at an opera or something. We knocked it out as fast/dynamic and faultless as possible but the reaction only came on the last song LORS when the crowd went bonkers, with this we did an encore and because the crowd had warmed up and continued with their enthusiasm and energy we ended up running through the whole set again and I believe that was the version used on the 12"."

"Never Mind Dirt - Here's The Bollocks" was produced by Pete Right and mixed at Southern Studios. It was during the recording that things came a bit unstuck.

Deno: "When Lou and Tim joined DIRT we loved them. Not the greatest rhythm guitar, but she could play, keep in time, create the required noise and was a lovely person and an asset to the band. Unfortunately Lou seemed to not have confidence in her own playing and during a live set would keep turning her amp down. Gary needed the wall of sound the rhythm guitar should create and he would reach back and turn her amp up, but she would often return to turn it down again. Unbeknown to us Lou's guitar was not present on the live recording and what was there wasn't strong enough so when we came to listen to it at southern studios where it was being mixed by Pete a member of Crass, it was suggested that Gary re record the rhythm guitar to save on studio time as Lou was not available.

I can't remember when it was exactly, but at some point after that Lou had already been in talks with Flux and had been asked to join along with Tim, she then told us she was leaving DIRT once her place had been secured. To this day we hold no grudge about Lou, she was a great person, so we wished her well and even came to support her first gig with them. So I'm sorry to her if she felt she was excluded but it was never intentional."

The record was released on Crass Records (221984-7) in January 1983 after DIRT had come to an abrupt end only the month before at the big Zig Zag all-dayer when Fox publicly left the band.

"The Zig Zag all dayer - what a fantastic idea and an event to be part of and still talked about to this day- the day went well with it first being arranged to squat the Rainbow (I believe) but swiftly moved to the Zigzag when the police got wind of it to shut it down. As it was all kept hush and need to know basis, we had to move quickly and early to get in and barricade the doors, so I believe we were there around 8-9am that morning. We were told by Crass that all bands names had gone into a hat but unfortunately for us, our name was the last to be pulled putting us on one band after Crass and the final band of the evening. As you can imagine, none of us were happy about this as it was an extremely long day being there so early and not playing till almost midnight. Most people would need to get their last train home and would need to have left by then. Finally most people would see crass as the headline band and believe the show was over after they had played and exit the venue to catch their last train. We tried to get Crass to change their mind and allow us to go on earlier in the schedule but they insisted this was the fairest way to do this.

Fox's dad Leo had been our lighting engineer for our previous gigs and brought his own rig. Leo was a great guy and we loved having him as part of our set up, but there had been some controversy over the lights earlier on in the evening and this had also upset Fox and the rest of us.

When it finally came for our turn to play, we were exhausted and already upset. Then when the crowd had virtually disappeared and we had to play for the few remaining faces left, it became too much, Fox had let it get on top of him and he felt he did not want to continue the set and left the stage.

During the short set that we managed that night, I noticed to the right of the stage was a recognisable face, Stuart from Special Duties (in the next episode of DIRT to become our new drummer, although none of us knew it at the time)."

Perhaps an unlikely pairing (Special Duties are somewhat notorious for the anti-Crass position they took in 1982 when they recorded "Bullshit Crass" for Rondelet Music (ROUND 24)), Gary enlisted Stuart's help after putting together a new project that involved Honey Bane and Daryl Hardcastle from Omega Tribe. Sadly this faltered after only a few rehearsals. However, as luck should have it, after Deno and Vomit had returned to the fold, and with Paul on bass, they set off on a tour with Antisect and Crucifix, but that's a story for another time.

"Never Mind The DIRT - Here's The Bollocks" has the rare honour of being only the second follow-up record to be released on Crass Records.

A1 Death In Reality

A2 Slaughterhouse Rock

A3 Canvey Island

A4 Bully

A5 Unemployment

A6 Another Filled Hole

A7 Democracy

B1 Public Execution

B2 Lables

B3 6.35

B4 Master Race

B5 Land of the Rising Sun

Centerprise

Centerprise was a bookshop in Hackney (136–138 Kingsland High Street) in London's East End (1971–2012). "We were told in 1970 that a bookshop would never work in the East End because East Enders didn't read." remembers Robin Simpson. Undaunted, founders Glenn Thompson, Margaret Thompson, Ken Worpole and Anthony Kendle struck out at 32 Dalston Lane. It had a coffee bar and provided a place where people could play chess and read poetry. It provided welfare and legal advice and adult literacy classes and offered budding authors the opportunity to publish their own works. Ken Worpole: "To have all these different things under one roof – nobody had done that before. It was a magic mixture, if you like". They later moved premises to 136-138 Kingsland High Street.

It was a maelstrom of ideas and stood front and centre in Hackney's counter-cultural miasma. The borough's flotsam and jetsam met there.

Centerprise allowed political and community groups to use the building as a mailing address. Each group had its own individual mailbox. The Anarchist Communist Association had Box 2. The Apostles and later Academy 23 and UNIT had Box 4. Anti-Racist Action "An organisation not run by trendy middle class lefties or by guilty patronising farts. Or even by political parties." (The Apostles 1982) had Box 10. Spare Change Press had Box 26. Small Change was run by Robert Dellar. He of 'Straight Up' fanzine and Mad Pride and a familiar face at Wapping and Centro Iberico. Hackney Womens' Centre, Box 41 and Red Action, 45.

On November 1st 2012 due to an ongoing dispute with Hackney Council over its rent, the property was seized and Centerprise locked out.

Chats Palace

Chats Palace, 42-44 Brooksby's Walk, Hackney, London, E6 6DF.

Designed by Sir Thomas Edwin Cooper and built in 1913 under the auspices of wealthy philanthropist Andrew Carnegie, Homerton Library provided the people of the East End with the opportunity to better themselves. However by 1974 with the opening of a new public library on Homerton High Street, the building became redundant. By 1976 and a change of fortune it was renamed Chats Palace Arts Centre.

In the 1980s it became a hotbed of political ferment. Flux of Pink Indians played there (23/10/80) as did Poison Girls, The Cravats and Annie Anxiety (28/01/81), The Mob, Hagar The Womb and Youth In Asia (02/06/83), Poison Girls and The Mob (15/07/83), Poison Girls and Omega Tribe (10/08/83), Poison Girls, Omega Tribe and Toxic Shock (10/09/83), Poison Girls (10/08/84) and Poison Girls and Blyth Power (23/08/85).

It's 1972 and two women –.Olive Morris and Liz Turnbull, occupy a flat above a laundrette. The women in question were members of Brixton Black Panthers. One, Olive had a stubborn streak. A young black woman and fearless organiser. The building, 121 Railton Road, Brixton SE24. They resisted several attempts to evict them sometimes vigorously. They eventually decided to squat a council property at 64 Railton Road. Business properties are harder to defend. The 121 was where black bookstore Sabaar Bookshop got its start. 121 also functioned as the Brixton Black Panthers HQ. Olive was an active member until its dissolution.

The British Black Panther Movement was founded in 1968 by Nigerian novelist and playwright Obi Egbuna, broadcaster Darkus Howe, poet Linton Kwesi Johnson and Olive Morris. In December 1968 Egbuna was arrested after the police claimed he was hatching a plot to kill. In the interim Trinidadian Althea Jones became the Movement's leader. The British State upped the ante. In 1970 19 members of the British Black Panthers were arrested following a demonstration against the police. This followed a campaign of harassment by the Metropolitan Police against a Caribbean restaurant in Ladbroke Grove. Dubbed the Mangrove Nine (two of those charged with riot offences included owner Althea Jones-Lecointe and Darcus Howe) they were found innocent of all charges by a jury of their peers.

The BBP produced a newspaper called Freedom News. It also had a Youth League.

In 1973 it squatted 74 Railton Road. There it opened a black bookshop called Unity Bookshop. However it was destroyed after fascists set it ablaze.

That same year the BBP folded following an acrimonious split. Olive Morris died on the 12th of July 1979. She was 27.

Sometime in the late 1970s Sabaar moved to 378 Coldharbour Lane. Just as they did so anarchists who up until this point had been using Sabaar as a mailing address seized the advantage and quickly set about using the building for their own purpose - establishing an anarchist social centre. Some of those involved were veterans of other campaigns. In a protest against the GLC selling Council houses to private developers 50 squatters occupied Kilmer House in Kennington.

The Brixton riots came and went. Nocturnal Emissions recorded "Brixton Uprising" at Archway Studios, Atlantic Rd, Brixton, 14th April 1981 on the week the rioting took place April 10th to April 12th. It was released as a limited edition cassette (SRC11) April 2nd 2021 to mark the 40th anniversary of the live show.

However tensions remained high. The police chipped away at the centre's support.

Groups from across the anarchist divide made use of its ample facilities. Black Flag (the newspaper of the international Anarchist Black Cross from January 1971 under the editorial leadership of Albert Meltzer and Stuart Christie. In the 1980s copies were folded upstairs at the 121.), London Anarchist Black Cross, the Kate Sharpley Library (or KSL the Kate Sharpley Library is the holder of historical anarchist texts. Its collection contains 2,500 English language books and 4,000 pamphlets and newspapers. It was originally held at the 121 Centre. However after a police raid on the premises in 1984, it was moved to St George

Mansions. It currently resides at the home of Barry Pateman and Jessica Moran in California.), Brixton Squatters Aid (the publishers of anarchist squatter magazine Crowbar) and local branches of Direct Action Movement (DAM).

"There was a cafe, bookshop and regular benefit gigs ranging from punk to queercore."

On Friday the 16th of March 1984 Flowers In The Dustbin played in the basement. On the 11th of September 1987 Thatcher on Acid, Idiot Strength and Wat Tyler played a benefit in the basement for the 121. Elsewhere at the Centro Iberico May 2nd 1982 Conflict, Rubella Ballet, Assassins of Hope, Zounds and Amsterdamned played a benefit for the 121 Centre.

It attracted the ire of the police and Special Branch who monitored its mail. This included the use of undercover officers or "spy cops". Andy Davey (cover name Andy Coles), while his main objective was to embed himself in the South London animal rights movement (he skilfully infiltrated Brixton Hunt Sabs who regularly met at the 121) helped fetch food to and from New Covent Garden.

On the 25th of March 1984 200 police successfully evicted seven squatted terraced houses on Effra Parade off Railton Road after Lambeth Council abandoned its plans to evict the 121.

On the 14th of August 1984 50 police officers raided four squatted houses and the 121 under the pretext of searching for firearms. None were found. "At the bookshop they spent three hours going through everything, at times we were not able to get inside as the bomb squad went through with sniffer dogs. Anything 'bugs', drugs or "firearms" could have been planted by them as we were not able to follow their search. "Have you found the Nuclear weapons yet?" asked one shop worker as the cops stomped in the basement and up to the roof."

The cafe dished up cheap healthy nosh from food skipped from New Covent Garden.

In 1993 local Nazis tried to burn the 121 Centre to the ground. Twice!

In 1997–1999 Lambeth Council made renewed efforts to get the building

back. 121 went to court claiming 12 years adverse occupation... and lost. In February 100 people turned out to foil an eviction. Finally, after a six month stand-off on the morning of the 12th of August 1999 150 cops broke in and evicted the building's last few remaining occupants.

Housmans Bookshop and Peace News

Housmans is one of Britain's oldest radical bookshops.

In order to better understand its origins we need to go back to the summer of 1936 when the PPU (Peace Pledge Union) set up a temporary bookshop at 36 Ludgate Hill, London WC4. Peace News, which went on to became the official publication of the PPU, started publishing the very same year June 6th under the editorship of Humphrey Moore.

In 1943 more permanent lodgings were found when they relocated to a room in the PPU's headquarters at Dick Sheppards House, 6 Endsleigh Street, Bloomsbury WC1.

Dick Sheppard (1880-1937) was an Anglican priest. On the 16th of October 1934 he famously put pen to paper and wrote a letter to the Manchester Guardian inviting its readers to send him postcards pledging never to support war. To everyone's surprise 135,000 men responded to his call. The following July Sheppard called a demonstration at the Albert Hall and in May 1936 he co-founded the Peace Pledge Union with Labour Party leader and well known social reformer George Lansbury and Methodist minister, socialist and pacifist Donald Soper née Lord Soper.

On the 26th of October 1945 and at the behest of writer, playwright and younger brother of A. E. Housman, Laurence Housman (1865-1959), the PPU leased a bomb-damaged property (124 Shaftesbury Avenue W1) from Westminster Council. Laurence had been a lifelong supporter of social causes including women's suffrage. He imagined a shop that promoted "ideas of peace, [...] human rights and a more equitable economy by which future wars, and all their inherent suffering, might be avoided.". They named the property in his honour.

However after three years when the lease was up for renewal they couldn't afford to pay its new more expensive rates and it was forced to close.

Peace News registered Housmans Bookshop as an additional trading name. Without a physical space it continued to trade as a mail order company and in 1954 the very first edition of the Housman's Peace Diary was published.

In 1958 Peace News acquired a property at 5 Caledonian Road N1 after receiving a monetary gift of £5,700 from the Reverend Tom Willis of Hull. PN moved in to the upper floors while Housmans set down roots downstairs. It opened for business on the 21st of November 1959.

It was in the offices of Peace News in 1958 that artist Gerald Holtom did his very first sketches of the Nuclear Disarmament symbol.

In 1961 Peace News severed all official ties with the PPU.

Dick Sheppards House, 6 Endsleigh Street, Bloomsbury

In 1974 it moved to new offices in Nottingham. The same year the IRA blew up a post box outside Housmans. The first issue of the Campaign Against Arms Trade's newsletter, which had been posted just 10 minutes earlier, was destroyed. No one was injured.

Anarchist monthly Wildcat (1974–1975) was based at 5 Caledonian Road.

Four years later a letter bomb (from an alleged Nazi source) was sent to Peace News. Housmans assistant Stewart Porte was injured in the attack and had to be treated for burns to his face, hands and chest. The Socialist Workers Party and Anti-Nazi League were also targeted in the terror spree.

On the 26th of May 1979 Crass + The Epileptics and Poison Girls played a benefit for Peace News at the Conway Hall.

The War Resisters International is headquartered at 5 Caledonion Road.

Over the next 40 years Housmans and Peace News would play host to numerous groups including CND, Direct Action Committee Against Nuclear War, Gay Liberation Front, Animal Liberation Front, London Lesbian and Gay Switchboard, London Greenpeace and the McLibel Support Campaign.

In 1990 US fast food giant McDonalds served writs on five members of London Greenpeace(1972-2001). Paul Gravett, Andrew Clarke, Helen Steel, Dave Morris and Jonathan O'Farrell faced libel charges after distributing copies of a leaflet "What's wrong with McDonald's: everything they don't want you to know". Paul, Andrew and Jonathon apologised. Helen and Dave did not and decided to fight on. The two were denied legal aid and mounted their own legal defence. Despite all the odds with everything stacked against them the two campaigners distinguished themselves in and out of court and after two and a half years (making it the longest trial in British legal history) got a satisfying result. For McDonalds it was something of a PR disaster.

Peace News returned to London in 1990.

Today Housmans still stands as a beacon of hope.

The Red Lion, Gravesend

The Red Lion in Northfleet, Gravesend has been hosting live music since 1978 under the watchful eye of owner and music lover Terry Lee. Situated in an area surrounded by heavy industry - IPM Paper Mills, AEI Cables, Bowater Scotts and Blue Circle Cement Mills, it was a Hells Angels pub in the 1980s.

The Red Lion in Northfleet, Gravesend has been hosting live music since 1978 under the watchful eye of owner and music lover Terry Lee. It became a popular live venue with Conflict and Anthrax who had a local residency there every Tuesday. Some of these live dates included Conflict, Annie Anxiety and Anthrax (08/10/81 when Paco made his live debut), Conflict, DIRT and Anthrax (05/11/81), Hagar the Womb (1982), Conflict and Anthrax (18/05/82), DIRT (15/06/82), Subhumans, The Mob and Faction (24/08/82), Conflict, Rubella Ballet and The Committed (28/08/82), Flux of Pink Indians, DIRT, Annie Anxiety and Anthrax (27/08/82) and Conflict and Liberty (08/10/84). It was Liberty's second gig. It would be the first of many with Conflict. On 05/11/84 Liberty was joined by Blind Drunk, Defyance and Lowlife. 20/11/84 with Lost Cherrees.

It was on one of these early live forays that drummer John Jacobs of East End Oisters The 4 Skins (who'd been roadieing for Conflict) stepped in to the breach and replaced Kenny Barnes Conflict's original drummer, perhaps at one of their gigs in Eltham. John grew up on the same 'notorious' SE London estate as Colin and John Clifford. 4 Skin Pete Abbot also grew up on the Coldharbour estate SE9.

AOH played their last gig here in 82. Leon: "We hired a van for this gig and I think Ivan's dad drove it for us .

Most of the audience stood outside the pub while we played which upset us a bit so we ended up smashing our instruments at the end of our set .As we were doing our Who impression most of the crowd piled in to enjoy the chaos . Despite the fact that they had not appeared to be interested in us while we played ,at the end of the night lots of people were saying we had been the best band they'd seen for ages and that we must return to Gravesend again soon. This really cheered us up and left us with happy memories of Gravesend. We never played another gig as AOH but at least we went out with a bang."

The Glasshouse 10/05/84 and 04/06/84

The Glasshouse in Camden was one of several squats opened up by the Kafe Kollaps collective. On the 10th of May 1984 Crass played what would be their final hoorah in London alongside Flux of Pink Indians, Annie Anxiety and D & V. People recall fearing for their lives due to the flexing of the floor which was on an upper story.

I spoke to Flux frontman Col Latter aka Alan Latter about Flux of Pink Indians second performance at The Glasshouse. Col: "At the end of March 1984 we released a double album "The Fucking Cunts Treat Us Like Pricks". It was an abrasive, experimental assault on the ears with the idea that if the music was too hard to listen to people would concentrate on the lyrics. As we began to play the songs from the album at gigs that followed its release, we were often shouted down and would finish the new set early and get involved with a slanging match with the audience who weren't too happy that they were not hearing Tube Disaster.

After a run of gigs with a similar outcome we organised one at the Glasshouse in Camden on 4th June, where we had played a month earlier with Crass, Annie Anxiety and D & V. It was a squatted venue and bands played in a large upstairs room, probably holding two to three hundred people.

For this 2nd gig at the Glasshouse, as a reaction to our reception over the last few months of gigs, we decided to change everything. No songs from "Fucking Cunts", no Flux banners and turn the whole thing into a rock'n'roll circus. Point being (sarcastically), perhaps this is what people want. Playing with us would be Chumbawamba and D&V.

We went along to the Glasshouse a few days before the gig to check on the space below the hall where we would play. When Crass had played there in May the floorboards were actually jumping up and down with the weight and throng of the audience. Below the hall, to our surprise, there wasn't much keeping the floor above up and there was a drop of about fifteen feet. How with the weight and movement of all those people it didn't fall through I will never know. We went and got some Acrow Props to support the beams and this fixed the bouncy floor problem !

For the gig, I drove over to the East End on my motorbike to pick up some dry ice for our set, amusingly it started to defrost as I drove back. At the hall we decided to put up tin foil to cover the back of the stage instead of our usual banners and we said to the guy doing the lights, do whatever you like. I can't remember how we all dressed but I wore shorts, t-shirt and sunglasses. I remember after the first song that I took the sunglasses off to get a better view of everything but things looked better with them on. We had re-worked our songs with an excellent slowed down rock section for 'Progress' and in another song I introduced each member of the band who then 'performed' a solo of some kind. Derek was a little self conscious with his solo and pretty much closed his eyes and just twanged all the strings of his bass together.

The whole set went down a storm and we'd never enjoyed ourselves so much on stage I don't think.

After our set we went backstage and it certainly sounded out in the hall that we had to go back on for an encore. Derek had recently been to see Miles Davis and quickly told us that Miles Davis had come back on for his encore starkers with only a saxophone covering his 'modesty' announcing that he wanted to strip jazz back to its bare roots. Derek suggested that we go back on starkers and declare that we wanted to strip punk back to its bare roots. We were all totally up for it and started to strip off. Of course this was not good for Lu who started to call us bastards. In hindsight the idea was not good and put her in a very awkward position as she obviously wouldn't strip off like the rest of us. We went back on in just our pants and I announced down the mic that we wanted to strip punk back to its bare roots. I remember seeing people towards the back straining to see above the people in front's heads to see if we had come back on completely naked.

I think we all felt that after this gig we couldn't go back to playing gigs in the way we had before. But we had to, this was a one off, and on 11th July we played in Aberdare with Crass, which turned out to be their last gig and then a tour kicking off on 19th August at Conway Hall in Holborn with Chumbawamba, KUKL and D&V."

Surbiton Assembly Rooms 09/05/85

Icons of Filth. Photo Paul Cussens.

On Thursday the 9th of May 1985 a riot took place outside a Conflict gig at Surbiton Assembly Rooms, Maple Road, South West London. Icons of Filth, Legion of Parasites, Stigma, Admit You're Shit and Lost Cherrees were also on the bill. Conflict had previously played there with Lost Cherrees and 3D Scream on 06/09/84 without incident. The gig was organised by Conflict and Jungle Records impresario Steve Brown.

Trouble flared towards the end of the gig after Conflict's equipment failed. Punks exited the building where there was a scuffle with police. Fans barricaded the entrance. The Special Patrol Group were called in to help stem the violence. 24 arrests were made. Colin Conflict was one of those arrested. Nine were given custodial sentences (Mike from Assassins of Hope was sentenced to three months in a young offenders institution + a soapy-spiked punk called Gordon who used to bunk up with the Hackney Hell Crew) and two were remanded in custody. Jungle Records were sent a bill by Kingston Council for damages to the hall.

Tony Lynch was there. "It was just a gig...but by the end of it...it was a full-on barricaded-in....'Us and them' confrontation with the police who turned up (without tickets for the gig....such a simple thing to buy the 1.75p ticket and come on in boys! So their attitude to a load of rabble invading a lovely woking-9-to-5-law-abiiding-London-affluent-surburb sent shock waves down their conformist spines and truncheons.

193

Stigma. Photo Paul Cussens.   *Icons of Filth. Photo Paul Cussens.*

They turned up and wanted to smash the gig up...end it there and then...despite the councils giving approval for Conflict to book and then advertise and then play it...!! So the atmosphere went from Punk gig to aggresion from their actions (which always provoke a counter reaction of course). The gig ended as there was a set of doors attempted to be barricaded up from the inside and a set-to was in order from then on in. The bands were in it aswell...Colin was infuriated up to the hilt about them coming smashing up the gig and trying to end it because ´they can´...as simple as that! So only about 50 or so of the (I would guess maybe 150 or 200 people there that night) were ´involved´ (I use that term loosely as...to be ´involved´ was simply just being in that corridor at the right or wrong time (depending on your point of view!). The gig was great musically and such a sad end to a corker evening..big stage and plenty of good viewing of the bands playing etc. I left out the back (as that was the only way to go home by then!) and saw the ´two sides´ playing out there parts much as you would expect...both were over-excited....one had the ´law´ (or laws) on their side...the other had the law on their backsides. It need not have happened at all...Conflict and the bands on the bill all turned up just to play their music and use the right of free speech...the police were trying and (they were successful in) stopping a band doing this that night."

Lee House

Lee House is a Grade ll listed building at 6a Rectory Road, Hackney N16. It was named after actor, theatre manager and pantomime writer Richard Nelson Lee (1851–1872). It was squatted in September 1988. Those who occupied it quickly set about establishing a fully functioning social centre. Its services included a bookshop (open Tuesday to Saturday 11am–6pm), a vegan cafe (open Thursday to Sunday 3pm–8pm), video screenings Tuesdays and Thursdays from 8pm and a skateboard ramp for local children to the rear of the house.

Lee House Centre is where Active Distribution (an anarchist publishing house and seller of radical books, publications, Sunrise t-shirts and H/C punk records run by Jon Elliott) got its start.

Spy cop John Dines (cover name John Barker) lived at Lee House and helped build the 7 foot half pipe. Dines is perhaps best known for eliciting a relationship with activist and future McLibel co-defendant Helen Steel after successfully infiltrating London Greenpeace. The relationship lasted two years before he eventually hightailed it and fled to South Africa looking for a better life. At least that was his cover story. He was eventually 'outed' in 2010.

In August 1989 Hackney council began moves to evict the squatters. "Well Hackney Council decided to evict it at the end of last August, though recognising it did provide services to the local community, claimed they (social services), had no other empty buildings in the area (bullshit). The place was going to be turned into a day centre for disabled people meant that it was decided to not resist eviction permanently, but to show token resistance as protest against the council's policy of cutting services.

There was a lot of leaflets distributed around London & the rest of the country asking for help, though by the night before the amount turned up was depressingly small. The building was barricaded, and things prepared to chuck at bailiffs etc. Not quite sure what (if anything?) was decided at the meeting. Next morning only one (top) bailiff turned up, with someone from the council, got a bucket of nasty things emptied over his head, banners went out, leaflets explaining situation given out to passers by & the media contacted. Bailiff went off to clean up after threatening to come back later with lots more.

The councillor hung around looking pissed off & even more pissed off when she got paint chucked at her. Rest of the morning was fairly uneventful. At about 1 o'clock there was no sign of reinforcements so it was decided to go down to Hackney town hall & occupy it. The decorators in the hall next to the balcony were given the afternoon off and the doors blocked up. Banners put out and lots of noise made, it got reports on south east TV and some local newspapers and the pigs got everyone after a couple of hours with no arrests." Raising Hell #21 1990.

On the 23rd of August 1981 The Mob, The Astronauts and Zounds joined a Summer Festival of music and mime at Parliament Hill Fields Adventure Playground, Highgate Road NW5. The music was provided courtesy of Street-Level Studios and Fuck Off Records. Also on the bill were 012 (Kif Kif aka Keith Dobson and Grant Showbiz. LP "Let's Get Professional" from 1984 features the artwork of Stephen 'Wilf' Wilmott who's perhaps most famous for his celebrated work for The Mob.), King Trigger, Blue Midnight (Grant Showbiz), The Entire Cosmos (J.B. aka

Jonathan Barnett) and Murphy Federation. The Mob's Joseph Porter took over drumming duties after a spell with The Entire Cosmos with whom he recorded a cassette with Here & Now called "The Hitch-Hikers Guide To The Entire Cosmos" on Fuck Off Records in 1980. It was a benefit for Retford CND. Plus the Street Level EP on Fuck Off Records (FEP002) October 1980 with Vince Pie and the Crumbs, Blue Midnight, The Voletones and The Entire Cosmos.

What marks the festival as significant is that it was the very first time the Puppy Collective saw The Mob play live. A pivotal moment if you will. Al Livingstone: "Indeed, what a great gig. Where we met Min as well. And had fun, fun, fun, fun, fun, all summer long."

100 Club 11/12/84

On the 11th of December 1984 Conflict headlined a show at the 100 Club. Joining them on the bill that day were Legions of Parasites, Icons of Filth, Exit-Stance, AYS and Living Legends (Ian Bone's musical troupe).

Class War stirred the pot by urging fans to smash up Oxford Street before things went awry. People exiting the gig were met by throngs of police and SPG vans, funnelling everyone towards Tottenham Court Road underground. Anyone stepping off the pavement or choosing to take a different route was pushed back. Par for the course if you saw Conflict then. Trouble seemed to follow the band wherever they went. Notwithstanding the ever present threat of Nazi boneheads. Sean Finnis from Exit-Stance does however make this astute observation. Sean: "We did some gigs in 1984 for the striking miners, at places like Scunthorpe and Chesterfield, plenty of miners turned up too, no trouble at those!" Thank you Sean.

Freedom Press

In May 1885, a "Circle of English Anarchists" led by Charlotte Wilson (a Cambridge graduate and political grandière and socialite) and comprising Nikola Chaikovski, Francesco Saverio Merlino and Russia's Peter Kropotkin, founded Freedom "A Journal of Anarchist Socialism" in September 1886. Wilson and Kropotkin along with Henry Seymour had previously co-edited "The Anarchist", Britain's first English speaking anarchist periodical. Freedom was printed at the offices of the Socialist League.

The lady grand edited, financed and published Freedom until she retired in 1895. The time was not conducive to anarchist ideas but new editor Alfred Marsh kept the ship afloat steering it through choppy waters.

After Max Nettlau and wealthy socialite Bernhard Kampffmeyer donated monies the Press obtained its own printing press and moved to new premises at 127 Ossulston Street (1894-1927). Donald Rooum: "In 1895, Charlotte Wilson resigned [as editor] and was replaced as publisher by Alfred Marsh, a violinist. In 1898, Freedom acquired its own printing facilities. The nieces and nephew of the artist Dante Gabriel Rossetti had been printing their own paper, The Torch, a journal of anarchist communism at 127 Ossulston Street, near Kings Cross, since 1885. In 1898 they decided to cease publication and arranged for the Freedom group to take over the premises. The Rossettis' printing equipment was bought and donated to Freedom by two sympathisers. Freedom Press stayed in Ossulston Street for the next 30 years."

In 1896 propagandist Thomas Cantwell became editor. In 1913 after Cantwell was incapacitated when he suffered a stroke and Marsh was forced to retire due to his failing health, compositor Tom Keell became acting editor.

It's 1914 and the outbreak of war led to an acrimonious split. Editor in chief and anti-militarist Tom Keell's hand was tried but he came out on top. Kropotkin, who supported the war effort in favour of an Allied victory, left the group.

The paper's anti-war stance attracted the ire of the State. Ossulston Street was raided by the authorities and on June 24th 1916 Keell and his companion Lilian Wolfe were tried under the Defence of the Realm Act and were imprisoned - Keel for two months and Wolfe for three.

After the war, anarchism was no longer in the ascendancy with the Bolsheviki gaining more traction both here and on foreign shores. To make matters worse Freedom was turfed out of 127 Ossulston Street. Keell soldiered on putting out an irregular bulletin.

However the Spanish Revolution of 1936 signalled an upward turn in the fortunes of the British anarchist movement. Front and centre was a fortnightly publication called "Spain and the World" (1936-1938). Founded by the son of anarchist militant Emidio Recchioni, Vero Recchioni aka Vernon Richards' newspaper was an instant hit. After just one issue it was taken on by Freedom Press. In 1939 after the defeat of the Spanish Republic it was renamed Revolt! before changing its name once again to War Commentary. War Commentary was published between 1939 and 1945.

In 1940 the first Freedom Bookshop was opened in Red Lion Passage. Unfortunately it was destroyed in an air raid in May 1941. It eventually set up home on Red Lion Street via Belsize Road in 1945.

However the group's anti-war work did not go unnoticed and in April of that year, four editors - Philip Sansom, John Hewetson plus Richards and his wife Marie Louise Berneri were arrested and charged under Defence Regulation 39a - conspiring to cause disaffection amongst members of the armed forces. They were each sentenced to nine months in prison though Berneri was allowed to go free as in the eyes of the law a wife could not be prosecuted for conspiring with her husband.

In December 1948 Berneri gave birth to a child who died shortly afterwards. Berneri died on the 13th of April 1949. She was 31.

In 1960 Freedom moved to Fulham. In 1961 Freedom Press began producing a new title - Anarchy. Edited by Colin Ward it ran from March 1961 until December 1970.

In 1963 Donald Rooum was fitted up for a crime he did not commit. Rooum was protesting Queen Frederika of Greece's visit to London when he was hit on the head by police officer Harold Challenor who then proceeded to plant a half-brick on Rooum's person. All charges were dropped after forensic evidence corroborated Rooum's version of events. He was paid £500 compensation.

Rooum, a cartoonist and self-confessed Stirnerite, developed a long working relationship with Freedom (and Peace News). In 1974 he created the character Wildcat for which he's best known. The feisty moggie first appeared in the pages of anarchist newspaper Wildcat (1974-1975) before finding a familiar home at Freedom in January 1980. The Wildcat strip ran until 2014. Donald died on the 31st of August 2019. He was 91.

In 1968 Richards purchased 84a and 84b Whitechapel High Street in Angel Alley. Express Printers got to work in the basement of 84a.

Vero eyed Albert Meltzer's proposal to hire a room at 84b with suspicion. This was not well received, setting them at loggerheads. It typified the political divide that existed between the two camps - class struggle anarchism v a more stuffy theoretical tradition. In 1970 Albert set about starting his own magazine (Black Flag).

Fast forward ten years. Vero hands over ownership of the building to a limited company Friends of Freedom Press.

In 1981 the print shop receives an upgrade. Aldgate Press is set up to replace the ageing Express Printers printing press.

A new young talent Nick Lant, who's art most people will be familiar with (Nick put his talents to work by drawing sleeves for four Subhumans discs - "Religious Wars" (SDL 7), "The Day The Country Died" (SDL 9), "Evolution" (FISH 2) and "Rats" (FISH 10) and the centre artwork for "Worlds Apart" (FISH 12) following a chance meeting. Atop a letter he'd written to the band was a punk rocker's head he'd drawn. They were so struck by his skills that they asked him to do a drawing for Religious Wars which he did... for free. All he asked was that they buy him a beer.) drew six covers for Freedom - Vol 46 No 1 January 1985, Vol 46 No 5 May 1985, Vol 46 No 7 July 1985, Vol 46 No 9 September 1985, Vol 46 No 11 November 1985 and Vol 47 No 2 March 1986. To this day no one knows of his whereabouts.

The Raven was a quarterly magazine produced by Freedom Press 1987-2003. There were 43 issues.

In the 1990s Freedom became the target of repeated attacks by fascists Combat 18. Militant anti-fascism was on the rise and the fascists were eager to exact their revenge. The worst of these incidents occurred when hooded C18 Nazis wielding clubs entered the building intent on violence. They smashed anything to do with typesetting and left as quickly as they arrived. The attack featured on ITV's premiere current affairs programme World in Action, The Terror Squad April 19th 1993.

In March 1993 the building was firebombed.

On the 10th of December 2001, Vernon Richards passed away peacefully in Hadleigh, Suffolk.

On the 1st of February 2013 Freedom was set ablaze (by an unknown assailant) for a second time. "Firefighters were called to the shop at around 5:00am and had the fire extinguished shortly after 7:00am. Around 15% of the ground floor was damaged by the blaze according to London Fire Brigade."

A year later on the 1st March 2014 publication of Freedom ceased though it still has an online presence.

Electric Ballroom 03/03/84

The Electric Ballroom, 184 Camden High Street NW1 is a nightclub and popular music venue in Camden Town. Whilst it had a previous life as The Buffalo Club and The Carousel, in 1978 owner Bill Fuller and Frank Murray breathed new life in to the place.

The new refashioned Electric Ballroom became a major music attraction. The Vicious White Kids, Joy Division, Adam & The Ants and The Clash (15/02/80 and 16/02/80) played on its repurposed stage.

However for the purposes of this book let's look at 03/03/84 when Welsh anarcho-punkers Icons of Filth took to the stage at the Electric Ballroom alongside Conflict, Flux of Pink Indians and Hagar The Womb.

In 1999 BBP Records & Tapes in conjunction with Yellow Fever Records committed six tracks (from an earlier cassette release "Live, Abused & Unamused: Live At The Bier Kellar, Leeds 22/2/84/ Live At The Electric Ballroom, Camden 3/3/84" on BBP) to vinyl "Show Us You Care"(BBPV3/Yellow Fever YG1). The six tracks were as follows:

A1 Mentally Murdered

A2 Virus

A3 Asking Too Much

B1 Self-Styled Superiority

B2 Power For Power

B3 Show Us You Care

They were remastered by Sned at Flat Earth. Art was by Icons artist extraordinaire Squeal.

BBP (Big Banana Productions), 90 Grange Drive, Swindon, Wiltshire SN3 was a popular cassette label run by Gogs aka Stephen Parsons (22/03/66–24/12/12). The BBP Records and Tapes catalogue was an Aladdin's cave of must-have demos and live tapes including Scum Tapes. Gogs released 94 tapes and eight "proper" records.

Ian Bone: "If 'punk's not dead' its thanks to sellotaped pound coins and people like Steve Parsons who have had the patience and good humour to scrape the tape off."

Lastly let's look at one other gig of note when on the 4th of September 1986 Conflict put together another bill at the Electric Ballroom that included AYS (their very last live performance), Pink Turds In Space (filling in for the recently deceased Toxic Waste) and Stalag 17.

The Waste were also added to the bill, but because several members of the band were due to appear in court in the morning in relation to hunt sab offences, they couldn't.

Brutal System (from Belgium) were also slated to play but for reasons not known didn't either.

Two cassettes and a CDr documenting Conflict's performance have been released – Conflict "Electric Ballroom 86", Conflict "Live At The Electric Ballroom" (PALMI 6) 1992, and Conflict "Live At The Electric Ballroom" 2022.

Dickie Dirt's Warehouse

Dickie Dirt's Warehouse, 88 Denmark Hill SE5 was a discount jeans warehouse, 24th January 1981 until its closure. However the Triangle that it eventually vacated changed hands and had many faces before Dickie Dirt's came along.

In 1894 the Metropole Theatre opened its doors showing the latest West End productions.

In 1906 after a change in fortunes it changed its name to Camberwell Empire Theatre. It began screening films and in 1924 became the Camberwell Empire and in 1930 the New Empire Cinema.

In 1939 on the outbreak of war it was demolished and reopened as the Camberwell Odeon on the 20th of March 1939 until the 5th of July 1975 when it eventually closed.

In August 1984 squatters occupied number 88 afore Stop The City (STC) 27th September. A benefit for STC Bust Fund Network 26/09/84 with Subhumans. Danbert Nobacon, Conflict, Eat Shit, Toxic Waste and Stalag 17 took place under its roof followed by a second benefit gig the following day (28/09/84) with Serious Drinking, Union of Fear, Ring and Panik Sphere.

Earlier that summer Subhumans frontman Dick Lucas scribbled down a lyric to a song called "Rats". "Rats" (B2) was a track on their 1984 EP Rats (released September 28th). The song is about STC and wonderfully captures the bravery and "enterprise" of those who dared to challenge the might of capital.

At one point in the thick of the action Dick overheard a cop in the scrum shout: "If you act like rats, you'll get treated like this... " which made its way in to the song and gave it its title.

If you act like rats you get treated like this, Said a policeman like we didn't exist

The song is a powerful call to action.

Skull Side

A1 Joe Public

A2 Labels

Bluurg Side

B1 When The Bomb Drops

B2 Rats

Rats have all gone underground

But we'll be back again next time 'round

We'll be back again next time 'round

We'll be back again

We'll be back again

We'll be back again

We'll be back again

Next time 'round

Next time 'round

Next time 'round

Next time!

On the 3rd of October 1984, police, builders and bailiffs evicted Dickie Dirt's. The building's owners even turned up in a Rolls Royce to watch the spectacle. However despite all their best efforts squatters reoccupied the building until it fell in to disrepair and was demolished in the spring of 1993 when it was replaced by accommodation for the homeless called 'The Foyer'. Today it's a fast food restaurant.

The Ad-Lib Club

The "Ad-Lib Club", The Kensington, 54 Russell Gardens W14 (1973–1985) was run by the Windsor Chapter of the Hell's Angels. Their headquarters was in Maidenhead Road. Russ Schnell: "I remember loads of bikers doing security and the cops who usually showed up to hassle punks staying well away the couple of times I went there."

It became something of a punk go-to venue. Some of the gigs that took place there included:

07/09/84 Sunglasses After Dark

06/10/84 Conflict, Icons of Filth and Exit-Stance.

Craig Thompson: "The place was rammed and it really did feel like we could change things and it was more like a political rally than a gig!"

09/1/84 Chaos, Satellites and Worms

13/11/84 Lost Cherrees, Karma Sutra and Rachels Pilchards

31/05/85 Conflict, Liberty and AYS

Mick Harrington: "I think we played there in 85 with Conflict & AYS, I remember a skinhead at the front eating a beer can, mad venue."

About David Insurrection

David Insurrection was born in 1962 and raised in NE Scotland. He's married with one daughter. At the age of 17 in the autumn of 1979 he discovered punk rock. It would leave a lasting impression on him. In 1980 he first heard Crass. That experience changed everything and would determine the direction his life took from that point onwards. In 1984 he began to identify as an anarchist and took his first activist steps. By this time he had immersed himself in everything anarcho-punk. In 1988 he produced his first zine. His next zine in 1990 was called Insurrection. In 1993 he moved to London. He stayed there for four and a half years returning to his native Scotland in 1997. It was during his stay in London that he first got a hankering for writing a book on anarcho-punk. He's still involved in the scene to this day.

THE FIRE STILL BURNS

Music inspired by the post-punk message

By David Gamage

THE FIRE STILL BURNS:
MUSIC INSPIRED BY THE POST-PUNK MESSAGE

WRITTEN BY DAVID GAMAGE

AND INSPIRED BY MANY

ADVENTURES IN A
D.I.Y. SCENE
DAVID GAMAGE

WWW.EARTHISLANDBOOKS.COM

RUNNING AT THE EDGE OF THEIR WORLD : THE SUSPECT DEVICE FANZINE STORY BY TONY AND GAZ SUSPECT

The behind-the-scenes story of one of the U.K.'s longest running, and best loved punk fanzines. From the typewriter set, cut and paste layouts, to the illicit night-time, photocopying, up to today's comparatively slick output. The book is filled with stories right from the very beginning of the community they helped build and support, and still do. It's about the changes and challenges Tony and Gaz had to overcome, and the lifelong friendships created in the process.

This book is about the Suspect Device fanzine, but it's also about the punks who came together to create the scene based on the principles of DIY, friendship and co-operation.

You'll love it, and it may even inspire you.

As the foreword from Pete Zonked says, "Get off your ass and do something."

AVAILABLE NOW AT: WWW.EARTHISLANDBOOKS.COM

THE REVOLUTION WILL BE TELEVISED

RAY STUART

Ray wrote 'The Revolution Will Be Televised' because he finally realised that if our present government wasn't going to trigger open rebellion, then nothing would.

Instead, he has embraced his middle-class roots; where he used to be full of passion and rage, he is now full of artisan bread and locally sourced cheese. Meat may be murder but so are his knees. He's leaving the street fighting and statue tipping to the young. Instead 'The Revolution Will Be Televised' is an appeal to people from all backgrounds, to imagine and work for a better, fairer society without the reliance on the straightjackets of traditional left-right politics or inherited privilege.

An important book in changing times, available now, direct from Earth Island Books, or any good book or record shop, or online retailer.

Remember, in this age of media, 'The Revolution Will Be Televised'.

EARTH ISLAND BOOKS

WWW.EARTHISLANDBOOKS.COM

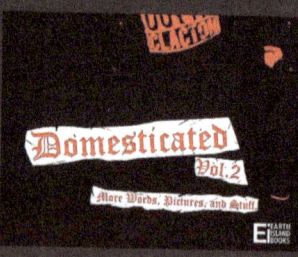